The Money Confidence Personality Quiz

What's Your Money Confidence Personality?

Before we dive in, let's get personal. Your relationship with money is unique—and understanding your money personality is the first step to building financial confidence.

Take the **Money Confidence Personality** Quiz to uncover:

- Your dominant money personality and how it impacts your financial decisions.
- The biggest challenge holding you back from true wealth.
- Your next best step to build lasting financial confidence.

Scan the QR code below to take the quiz now!

(Once you complete the quiz, you'll receive your personalized result and action steps to help you start making confident money moves right away!)

THE Money CONFIDENCE CODE

JANEIL PIERRE

Manufactured in the United States of America

ISBN: 979-8-9988107-2-5

Library of Congress Control Number: 2025906176

Follow Janeil Pierre

Social Media Outlets:

Facebook: https://www.facebook.com/janeilpierre
Instagram: https://www.instagram.com/janeilpierre/
LinkedIn: https://www.linkedin.com/in/janeil-pierre/
TikTok: https://www.tiktok.com/@janeilpierre

CONTENTS

Foreword

There's a moment when everything changes—when you realize that your relationship with money is actually a reflection of your relationship with yourself. I've lived this truth. I've taught this truth. And in "The Money Confidence Code," Janeil Pierre masterfully guides readers through this profound awakening.

I remember standing on stages around the world, teaching about transformation, and noticing a pattern. No matter how much confidence people built in other areas of their lives, money often remained their final frontier of fear. They could speak with authority about their expertise, lead with conviction in their careers, and even transform their relationships—but their financial voice still shook. Their money story still held them captive.

This is why "The Money Confidence Code" isn't just another book about money. It's a soul-deep exploration of worth, voice, and transformation. As someone who has spent decades helping people step into their power, I recognize the unique magic Janeil brings to the financial conversation. She understands that true financial freedom isn't just about numbers—it's about healing, growth, and claiming your worth.

When Janeil first shared her framework with me, I was struck by how it addressed the missing piece in financial education. While most experts focus on what *to do* with your money, Janeil helps you understand and transform who *you're being* with your money. Her approach bridges the gap between knowing and doing; between information and transformation.

Through The Confidence Money Method™, Janeil offers what so many financial books miss: a pathway to transformation that honors both your bank account and your soul's journey. She guides you through understanding your money story, claiming your worth, finding your financial voice, and creating a legacy that extends far beyond your own life.

What makes this work so powerful is its ability to meet you exactly where you are while calling you into your highest potential. Janeil doesn't shame you for where you've been or judge you for your current reality. Instead, she helps you understand how your past has shaped your present and then provides you with the tools to create a new future.

I've witnessed countless transformations in my career, and I recognize in these pages the same elements that create lasting change: truth-telling, deep understanding, practical application, and unwavering support. Janeil weaves these elements together masterfully, creating a journey that's both challenging and nurturing.

What you hold in your hands is more than a book—it's an invitation to rewrite your money story. Through Janeil's guidance, you'll discover that financial empowerment isn't about following someone else's rules; it's about finding your authentic voice and truth. You'll learn that wealth building isn't just about accumulation; it's about alignment. And you'll understand that your financial journey isn't just about you; it's about the legacy you're creating for generations to come.

As you turn these pages, prepare to be challenged, inspired, and transformed. Janeil doesn't just tell you what to do; she walks beside you as you uncover your own power to create lasting change. She shares not only her expertise but also her heart, creating a safe space for your transformation to unfold.

In a world where money conversations often focus on lack and limitation, Janeil brings a message of possibility and empowerment. She shows us that financial confidence isn't something we need to earn—it's something we need to claim. She demonstrates that our worth isn't measured by our net worth, but our net worth often reflects our sense of worth.

Your relationship with money is about to transform. Your voice is about to get stronger, your worth is about to expand, and your future is about to get bigger than you've ever allowed yourself to imagine.

Welcome to your financial awakening. Welcome to "The Money Confidence Code."

Lisa Nichols
Motivational Speaker,
New York Times Bestselling Author, and
Star of "*When My Soul Speaks*" on Broadway

Introduction:
The Money Confidence Code

The numbers on my bank statement weren't the problem. They never were.

Standing in that luxury resort bathroom in spring 2024, fixing my lipstick alongside a stranger named Shana, I finally understood what had been missing from every conversation about money I'd ever had. As a financial coach, I'd spent years teaching people about budgets, debt repayment strategies, and savings plans. But here was Shana—a brilliant nurse with an entrepreneurial dream—saying words that would transform my entire approach to financial freedom:

"I want to build a business, but I just don't believe I deserve wealth."

In that moment, everything clicked. The reason why so many intelligent, capable people struggle with money isn't about knowledge—it's about confidence. It's about believing you deserve more. It's about trusting yourself to make powerful financial decisions. It's about knowing, deep in your bones, that you are worthy of abundance.

You might be wondering if this is just another financial advice book. It's not.

Look around. We're drowning in financial information. The internet is bursting with budgeting, credit, investing, saving, and debt repayment tips. Social media influencers promise get-rich-quick schemes left and right. Financial gurus shout contradicting advice from every corner of YouTube.

Yet, despite all this available information:

- According to the FINRA Foundation's 2022 study, 53% of Americans feel anxious when thinking about their finances

- The TIAA Institute's 2023 Personal Finance Index reveals Americans correctly answer only 48% of financial literacy questions

- A 2023 Bankrate survey shows 68% of Americans couldn't cover living expenses for one month if they lost their primary income

- According to the American Psychological Association's 2023 survey, 83% of Americans report money as a significant source of stress

Why? Because information alone isn't enough.

What Makes This Book Different

You might be wondering how this book is different from the countless other financial advice books on your shelf. Here's what makes "The Money Confidence Code" unique:

1. Integration of Psychology and Financial Literacy: While most financial books focus solely on strategies and systems, this book addresses the deeper psychology that drives your money decisions. We explore how your worth, voice, and vision shape your financial reality.

2. Transformation vs. Information: Traditional finance books give you more knowledge; this book guides you through actual transformation. Instead of just learning about money, you'll experience a fundamental shift in how you relate to wealth.

3. The Confident Money Method™: Unlike generic financial advice, this method provides a clear pathway that integrates:

   - Healing your money stories
   - Finding your financial voice
   - Building unshakeable confidence
   - Creating lasting transformation

4. Practical Spirituality: While many books focus either on practical tips or spiritual abundance, "The Money Confidence Code" bridges this gap. You'll learn how to combine practical financial strategies with deeper spiritual principles.

5. Experience-Based Wisdom: This isn't theory - these principles emerged from real transformations with thousands of clients. You'll find authentic stories, practical examples, and proven strategies that have created lasting change.

I learned these lessons the hard way. Before becoming a Neuro-transformational Life and Financial Coach, I slept on an air mattress in a cramped apartment shared with seven others, wondering if I'd ever break free from financial struggle. I had read all the books and knew the strategies, but something was missing.

That missing piece? Financial confidence.

When you lack financial confidence, it seeps into every corner of your life:

You stay in jobs that drain your soul because you don't believe you deserve better.

You avoid looking at your bank account because every number feels like a judgment.

You make decisions from a place of fear rather than empowerment.

You shrink your dreams to fit your current circumstances.

You accept less than you're worth because asking for more feels impossible.

But here's what I've discovered through helping thousands of clients transform their financial lives—financial confidence is like a key that unlocks doors you didn't even know were closed. When you believe in your ability to manage money, trust your financial decisions, and know your worth, everything changes.

The Money Confidence Code isn't about complex investment or extreme budgeting tactics. Instead, it's a revolutionary approach that transforms your relationship with money from the inside out.

This journey begins with one crucial truth: Your self-worth isn't measured by your net worth.

In the chapters ahead, you'll meet people like AJ, who saved her first $20,000 in one year after years of failed attempts at saving. You'll learn from Cora, who doubled her freelance rates when she finally understood the true value she provides. You'll discover how Dr. Fran restructured her financial plan to eliminate over $600,000 worth of debt by trusting her own intuition.

Their stories could be your story. Their transformations could be your transformation.

This book is for you if:

> You're tired of knowing what to do but struggling to actually do it.
>
> You make good money but still feel anxious about your finances.
>
> You want to build wealth without sacrificing everything you enjoy.
>
> You're ready to transform your relationship with money from the inside out.
>
> You know you're capable of more, but something keeps holding you back.

The path to financial freedom isn't just about strategies and systems—it's about believing you deserve to walk that path in the first place. It's about building the confidence to take decisive action, make bold decisions, and create lasting change.

Are you ready to transform your relationship with money? To step into a new level of financial confidence? To create a life where money supports your dreams instead of limiting them?

Turn the page. Your transformation begins now.

When Money Speaks to Your Soul

Just as every person has a story waiting to be told, your money carries messages waiting to be heard. These messages aren't just about dollars and cents—they're about worth, possibility, and the future you dare to create.

Like the stories we keep in our vault, sometimes our deepest money truths are the ones we're most afraid to face. But everything changes when we find the courage to hear, and listen, to what our money is trying to tell us.

I've seen this transformation countless times. As an executive producer of Lisa Nichols' Broadway debut, *When My Soul Speaks*, I'm reminded that our greatest breakthroughs come when we dare to share our truth. Your money story is no different. It's waiting for you to step onto your own stage, claim your financial voice, and speak your truth into existence.

Welcome to "The Money Confidence Code."

A Note About This Book

Each chapter builds upon the previous one, creating a complete system for financial transformation. You'll find:

- Real stories from people who've transformed their financial lives
- Practical exercises to build your financial confidence
- Action steps to implement what you learn
- Reflection questions to deepen your insights
- Tools and templates to support your journey

Don't just read this book—engage with it. Do the exercises. Answer the questions. Track your progress. The more you participate in your transformation, the more powerful your results will be.

Remember: This isn't about becoming perfect with money; it's about becoming confident with money. It's about creating a financial life that feels good—one that supports your dreams, aligns with your values, and allows you to show up fully in the world.

Your financial transformation starts here.

This book is dedicated to my heavenly grandmother, Juliet Pierre Roberts. Thank you for being the best grandmother a little girl could ever ask for. Continue to sleep peacefully, Mammie.

PART 1: HEARING THE CALL

CHAPTER 1

Your Money
Is Speaking

The music faded into the background as I stood in line at the grocery store, my heart pounding so loud I could barely hear the steady beep of items being scanned. *Lord, please don't let this bill be more than thirty dollars*, I silently prayed, not realizing I was holding my breath. The small pile of groceries looked pitiful on the conveyor belt—a loaf of bread, some peanut butter, a bag of rice, the cheapest vegetables I could find… Barely enough to last the week, but there I was, hands trembling as I waited for the cashier to announce my total.

Time seemed to slow down with each item she scanned. *Beep*. A can of tuna. *Beep*. Store-brand pasta. *Beep*. The last few bananas from the discount produce section. My stomach clenched as the numbers on the display crept upward: $12.47… $18.92… $24.35…

It wasn't just about the money. It was about what that number would say about me. About my life. About how close I was to the edge. I needed food, yes, but I also needed to not run out of money before my next paycheck. One unexpected expense, one miscalculation, and the careful house of cards I'd built would come tumbling down.

"That'll be twenty-eight dollars and seventeen cents," the cashier announced. Relief flooded through me so intensely that my knees went weak. I handed over my card, praying again, this time, that it would go through. When it did, I gathered my bags with shaking hands, fighting back tears that threatened to spill over.

It wasn't until I had trekked halfway up the ice-covered block that I realized something: my money had been screaming at me that entire time. Not about the groceries or the total, but about something deeper. Something I'd been too scared to hear.

Have you ever noticed how money speaks? Not in the rustle of dollar bills or the ping of a deposit notification but in the whispers of your hesitation before making a purchase? In the knot in your stomach when checking your bank balance? In the way your voice shakes when asking for a raise you know you deserve?

Your money is speaking. It has been all along.

But, like many of us, you've probably been taught to listen to everything except what your money is truly saying. You've been told to focus on budgets and spreadsheets, to follow rigid rules and systems, to push aside your feelings, and to "just be logical" about your finances.

Yeah, how's that working out for you?

The Language of Money

Have you ever followed all the "right" financial advice only to feel like something was still missing? That's because traditional financial wisdom often speaks a language that misses half the conversation.

Most financial advice treats money like it's just mathematics—a simple equation of income minus expenses. "Spend less than you earn." "Save 20% of your income." "Follow the 50/30/20 rule." These guidelines sound logical, simple even. But if money were just math, wouldn't we all be wealthy by now? The emptiness comes from treating your financial life like a spreadsheet while ignoring the human being who has to live it.

We're told budgets fail because we lack discipline or need a better system. But here's the truth: budgets fail because they try to solve an emotional problem with a logical solution. It's like trying to heal a broken heart by creating a relationship spreadsheet. When your spending is driven by unmet needs, childhood patterns, or deep-seated fears, no amount of categorical planning will address the root cause. Budgets aren't terrible tools—they're just the wrong tools for the real problem.

This isn't just theory. According to a 2023 Capital One study, 77% of Americans report that their emotions impact their financial decisions. Our relationship with money goes far deeper than logic.

Picture this: Your spreadsheet shows you can afford something, but your stomach tightens at the thought of buying it. Or the numbers say you should be fine, but you still lie awake at night worrying about money. That's because spreadsheets can't account for your mother's voice in your head about money being scarce, or the shame you feel about past financial mistakes or the way you use shopping to feel more in control. Numbers can track your spending, but they can't heal your relationship with money.

You know you should save more. You understand compound interest. You've read the books and taken the courses. Yet, somehow, you keep finding yourself in the same financial patterns. This isn't a failure of knowledge—it's a disconnect between your intellectual understanding and your emotional reality. When your conscious mind says "save," but your subconscious mind says "I don't deserve abundance," guess which one usually wins?

This is why we need to learn a new way of working with money—one that speaks to our spreadsheets and souls. Your money is trying to tell you something deeper than "income minus expenses equals cash flow." It's speaking a language that includes emotions, energy, and inherited patterns.

When you learn to understand this broader language of money, something profound shifts. Your financial choices begin to align naturally with your values, your numbers start reflecting your true needs, and the constant battle between what you know you "should" do and what you actually do begins to dissolve.

Money As Energy

Think of the last time you handed over money for something you truly valued. Maybe it was a gift for someone you love, an investment in your education, or a donation to a cause you believe in. Remember how that exchange felt different from paying a bill you resent or making a purchase out of guilt? Same dollars, completely different energy.

Money is like water; it can be frozen into static numbers in your bank account, or it can flow as a dynamic force through your life. It carries the energy of how it was earned, how it's kept, and how it is spent. Overtime pay, earned at a job you hate, feels different from the money earned doing work you love. The inheritance that came with strings attached carries a different weight than the bonus you earned through your own efforts. When you begin to sense these energy differences, you realize your bank balance is only part of the story.

Notice where money flows easily into your life—and where it feels blocked. Some people find it effortless to earn but impossible to keep. Others excel at saving but struggle to spend on themselves without guilt. These patterns aren't random. Money flows according to our deepest beliefs about what we deserve, what's possible, and what's "enough." The promotion you keep getting passed over for, the clients who don't pay on time, and the unexpected expenses that always seem to arrive just when you're getting ahead are not coincidences. They're showing you where energy is stuck.

Your financial behaviors create patterns, like trails in the snow. Every money choice leaves an energetic footprint. Consider what stories your patterns tell. The bills you pay first reveal what you truly value; the purchases you hide speak to your financial shame. The prices you'll negotiate (and the ones you won't) show your self-worth, while the money you'll spend on others, versus yourself, exposes your boundaries.

When you track these patterns, you begin to see the invisible choreography of your financial life. That cycle of feast and famine? It's showing you something about your relationship with security. The way money seems to burn a hole in your pocket? It's highlighting your relationship with abundance.

Your money is constantly sending you messages through its energy. Feel that pit in your stomach when you check your balance? That's a message. Notice the excitement that bubbles up about certain investments? That's a message. Pay attention to the resistance that surfaces when it's time to raise your rates—yes, that's a message, too. These aren't random emotional noise—your financial intuition is trying to get your attention. Just as physical pain tells you something's wrong in your body, financial discomfort points to places where your money's energy needs attention.

Learning to work with money as energy doesn't mean ignoring the practical aspects of financial management. Instead, it adds a crucial dimension to your financial awareness. When you understand money's practical and energetic aspects, something profound happens: Your decisions align logically and intuitively. You begin to identify and clear blocks to receiving. Your money patterns transform at their root, creating sustainable wealth that feeds your soul and your bank account.

The key is learning to sense and interpret these energy patterns. Just as a surfer learns to read the ocean's movements, you can learn to read the energetic currents of your financial life. This isn't mystical thinking—it's a practical skill that transforms your entire relationship with money.

Your Money Voice

Just as each person has a unique speaking voice, we each have a distinct way of expressing ourselves through money. This is your money voice; the complex melody of earning, spending, saving, and sharing your financial resources.

Listen closely to how you talk about money. Do you speak in terms of scarcity ("I can't afford that") or abundance ("I'm choosing to invest elsewhere")? Your words reveal your deeper financial beliefs. Some of us whisper about money, afraid to look at our bank accounts. Others shout through impulsive purchases or maintain a stern silence around financial matters altogether.

Money, like music, carries tone. Your financial tone might be anxious and staccato—quick purchases followed by buyer's remorse. Or perhaps it's hesitant and muted—keeping your prices low and apologizing for your rates. Maybe it's demanding and sharp—spending to prove your worth. Understanding your tone helps you recognize when you're speaking from habit rather than truth.

We learn our first money language at home, absorbing our family's financial dialect without realizing it. Perhaps you inherited your father's "save for a rainy day" mantra or your mother's "money is meant to be enjoyed" philosophy. Maybe your culture taught you that discussing money is taboo, or that specific careers are more "respectable" than others. These inherited patterns become your default money dialect until you consciously choose a new way to speak.

Your true money voice emerges when you align your financial choices with your values. It's the confidence to name your price without flinching, the peace of making purchases that reflect your priorities, and the clarity to say no to financial obligations that don't serve you. Like finding your speaking voice as a singer, discovering your authentic money voice requires practice, patience, and the courage to make some noise along the way.

The question isn't whether you have a money voice—you're already using it every day. The question is whether your current financial voice is genuinely yours or if you're still speaking in someone else's tone. What would it feel like to clear your financial throat and speak your truth about money?

The Hidden Conversations

Behind every financial decision you make runs a hidden conversation; a continuous stream of beliefs, stories, and patterns that shape your relationship with money. Like background music in a store subtly influencing what you buy, these invisible dialogues guide your financial choices without you even realizing it.

"Rich people are greedy." "You have to work hard for money." "There's never enough." These narratives run like old movies in the theater of your mind, coloring every financial scene you encounter. Perhaps you're replaying the memory of your parents arguing about bills or the shame of that time your credit card was declined. These stories aren't just memories; they're active scripts directing your financial decisions today.

Beneath your conscious thoughts about money lie deeper, often contradictory beliefs. You might intellectually know you deserve abundance while unconsciously believing staying small is safer. These hidden beliefs whisper constant messages: "Don't ask for more—you might lose what you have." "Success will change you." "Money corrupts." Until these whispers are brought to light, they'll continue to shape your financial reality.

Your relationship with money didn't start with you. You inherited financial patterns just as surely as you inherited your eye color. The way your grandmother hoarded resources during hard times might show up in your overstuffed pantry. Your father's feast-or-famine business cycle might appear in your work rhythms. These inherited patterns carry emotional DNA that influence your financial decisions today.

Ignoring these hidden conversations comes at a cost. It shows up as the endless cycle of financial decisions you regret but can't seem to change: the business that never quite breaks through, the savings that never quite grow, the debt that never quite disappears. Every unexamined belief, every inherited pattern left on autopilot, exacts its price—not just in dollars, but in dreams deferred and potential unrealized.

But here's the transformative truth: Once you become aware of these hidden conversations, they lose their subconscious power over you. Like turning on the lights in a dark room, awareness allows you to see what's really been directing your financial life. Only then can you choose which stories to keep, which beliefs to change, and which patterns to consciously reshape.

What hidden conversations are running in the background of your financial life? What would change if you finally heard them?

Transformational Moment: The Mirror Exercise

Take a deep breath. We're about to do something that might feel uncomfortable, but I promise it will reveal something powerful about your relationship with money. Find a quiet space where you won't be interrupted. Have your phone or computer ready, along with a journal and pen.

First, set an intention. This isn't about judgment or planning—it's about listening. We're creating space to hear what your money is trying to tell you.

Now, log into your bank account.

Notice your body's response before you even see the numbers. Are your shoulders tensing? Is your breathing shallow? Are you tempted to close this book? These physical reactions are part of your money story.

Look at your balance.

Stay with it. Don't click away. Don't start planning. Just observe what comes up and begin writing:

What's your first emotional response? Name it specifically—not just "bad" or "good," but "ashamed," "hopeful," "overwhelmed," "proud."

Where do you feel this in your body? Your chest? Your stomach? Your throat?

Now, look at your recent transactions. Each one tells a story:
Which purchases make you feel light? Heavy?
What patterns do you notice?
Which transactions trigger justification in your mind?
What do you wish was different?

Keep writing, letting your thoughts flow without censoring yourself. If you feel the urge to stop, that's normal. Stay with it.

Now, imagine your bank balance as a mirror. What is it reflecting to you about:

Your values?
Your fears?
Your unmet needs?
Your hopes?

Finally, write a letter from your money to yourself. What has it been trying to tell you? What wisdom does it hold? Let the words flow without editing yourself.

This exercise often brings up strong emotions. That's normal—even valuable. You're breaking the pattern of automatic reactions to your finances and creating space for new awareness to emerge.

Take a final deep breath. Close your banking app. Read what you've written.

Notice how this feels different from your usual money moments. You've just created a new pattern; one of presence and listening rather than reaction and avoidance. This is the beginning of a new conversation with your money.

Return to this exercise whenever you feel disconnected from your financial truth. Each time, you'll hear something new.

When Money Whispers

Listen closely to the phrases that slip from your lips about money. These common refrains aren't just casual comments—they're doorways into your deeper financial truth. Let's decode what your money is really trying to tell you.

"I Can't Afford It." Sometimes, this statement is a healthy boundary, a clear-eyed assessment of your current priorities. But often, it's fear wearing the mask of practicality. When you say these words, pause and ask yourself: Am I making a conscious choice about my resources, or am I letting old fears make the decision? The exact words can mean, "This isn't aligned with my values right now" or "I don't believe I deserve this." Which is true for you?

"I'm Bad With Money." This common self-accusation usually hides a deeper story. Perhaps you're actually quite skilled at earning but struggle with keeping. Maybe you're excellent at budgeting but resist looking at investments. "Bad with money" is a blanket judgment that obscures the actual pattern. What if you're not bad with money at all but rather working with financial systems that don't match your natural strengths?

"Money Is Hard." When this thought surfaces, it's worth asking: Hard compared to what? Often, this belief serves as a shield, protecting you from taking financial responsibility or risks. If money is "hard," you don't have to try. You don't have to change. But what if money isn't hard—what if it's simply unfamiliar? Like learning any new language, financial fluency comes with practice, not perfection.

"I'll Never Have Enough." This whisper often comes from an old wound; a time when there wasn't enough and scarcity left its mark. It can drive you to achieve but it can also keep you running on a hamster wheel of perpetual striving. Consider what "enough" truly means. Have you ever defined it? Sometimes, "I'll never have enough" is really saying, "I don't know how to feel secure," or "I'm afraid to stop proving my worth."

When heard with compassion, these money whispers can transform from limiting beliefs into valuable insights. They're not prophecies or final verdicts; they're invitations to deeper understanding. Next time you hear yourself speak these phrases, pause. Listen. Ask yourself:

What am I really saying about money? What am I really saying about myself? What new truth is ready to emerge?

Remember, these common money messages aren't random thoughts. They're clues leading you to your authentic financial voice. The key isn't to silence these whispers but to understand what they're really trying to tell you.

Learning To Listen

Like tuning into a faint radio signal, hearing your money's messages requires patience, practice, and a willingness to be still. This isn't about mastering spreadsheets or memorizing investment terms; it's about developing a deeper awareness of your financial frequency.

Most of us rush through our money moments—quickly swiping our cards, hastily checking balances, and automatically paying bills. But awareness grows in the pauses. Try slowing down your financial transactions. Before making a purchase, pause. Before checking your accounts, take a breath. Notice what emotions, sensations, and thoughts arise in these moments of stillness. These quiet spaces between financial actions often hold your most valuable insights.

Money consciousness isn't something you achieve once; it's a practice you return to daily. It might look like taking a moment to feel gratitude as you pay your bills, noticing your energy when you invoice clients, or observing your thoughts as you make spending decisions. Each conscious interaction with money builds your capacity to hear its deeper messages.

Your financial intuition is like a muscle; it strengthens with use. The power of this intuition isn't just theoretical. A 2023 study from the Journal of Behavioral Finance found that traders who trusted their intuition alongside analysis made 23% better investment decisions than those relying solely on analytics.

Your gut feelings about money aren't random. They're drawing on deep wells of experience and pattern recognition that your conscious mind might miss. That gut feeling about an investment, the subtle knowledge of when to save or spend, and the inner whisper about whether or not a purchase aligns with your values aren't random hunches; they're your financial wisdom speaking. The more you acknowledge and act on these subtle signals, the clearer they become.

Perhaps the most challenging part of learning to listen is trusting what you hear. Your inner financial wisdom might challenge conventional advice, guide you toward unexpected choices, or ask you to change patterns that feel safe, even if unfulfilling. Learning to trust this wisdom is like learning to trust your own voice—it requires courage, practice, and gentle persistence.

Perhaps begin with a daily money minute: sixty seconds of conscious attention to your financial energy. Notice how money flows through your day. Observe without judgment. Listen without attempting to fix or change anything. Just as meditation builds mindfulness, these small moments of financial awareness build your capacity to hear and trust your money's messages.

Remember, your money has been speaking all along. Your task isn't to make it speak louder but to become a better listener. What might you hear if you gave your financial life the same attention you give to a dear friend's words?

The Awakening

Sometimes, money has to shout before we finally hear it. Like a persistent friend trying to share an important truth, your finances have ways of demanding attention when whispers aren't working anymore. Recognizing these wake-up calls can transform what feels like a crisis into a catalyst.

That recurring overdraft fee isn't just about poor timing. The credit card balance that keeps you up at night isn't simply about overspending. Constantly worrying about your business finances, despite growing revenue, isn't merely anxiety. These persistent patterns are your money raising its voice, trying to cut through the noise of habits and assumptions to tell you something important.

Financial patterns tell stories. That mysterious ability to earn more but never seem to have more? It's speaking to your relationship with abundance. The way unexpected expenses appear just as your savings grow? That's revealing a belief about what you're allowed to keep. The clients who always haggle over your rates? They're reflecting your own doubts about your value.

What if your money stress isn't a problem to solve but a message to decode? That knot in your stomach when you think about retirement might be inviting you to face your fears about the future. The shame that surfaces when you make a large purchase could be highlighting where you need to heal your relationship with receiving. Even debt can be a teacher, showing you where you've been outsourcing your power.

Clarity begins with curiosity. Instead of pushing away financial discomfort, lean into it. Ask questions. Get curious about your patterns; notice what triggers money anxiety and what brings financial peace. Your awakening might start with something as simple as tracking your spending without judgment or writing down your earliest money memory. The goal isn't to fix anything yet—it's to understand.

This financial awakening isn't always comfortable. Like any growth, it might involve facing truths you've been avoiding or questioning beliefs you've long held sacred. On the other hand, however, there is the opportunity for a new relationship with money; one built on awareness rather than avoidance or consciousness rather than conditioning.

Remember, awakening is just the beginning. It's the moment you realize there's a deeper conversation happening with your money, and you finally decide to consciously participate. What messages have you been avoiding? What patterns are asking for your attention? What new understanding is ready to emerge?

Wealth Wisdom Reflection:
1. What is your money trying to tell you right now?
2. Which money messages feel inherited versus authentic to you?
3. Where do you feel most disconnected from your financial truth?
4. What would change if you truly listened to your money's wisdom?

A Voice Transformed

When A.J. first contacted me, her voice cracked with desperation. "I can't keep living like this," she confessed. Every month, I'm running out of money, charging essentials on credit cards, and watching my savings vanish the moment an unexpected bill appears." The cycle was crushing her spirit—save $500, watch it disappear, start over—again and again.

What A.J. craved wasn't just money in the bank—it was peace of mind—the ability to sleep at night knowing she could handle whatever life threw at her. But her money spoke a language of scarcity and survival, and she was too overwhelmed to hear anything else.

Through our work together, A.J. learned to listen differently. Instead of seeing her vanishing savings as failures, she recognized them as messages about where her financial foundation needed strengthening. We created a plan that spoke her language and acknowledged her fears while building her confidence.

A year later, my phone rang as I boarded a flight to Las Vegas. It was A.J., her voice now bursting with joy. "I did it!" she exclaimed. "Twenty thousand dollars in savings—for the first time in my adult life!" The number itself wasn't what brought tears to her eyes. It was what that number said: "You're safe. You're secure. You can trust yourself with money." Her money was still speaking. But now, finally, she knew how to listen.

Your money has always been speaking. It's been trying to guide, teach, and help you grow. The question isn't whether your money has something to say—it's whether you're ready to listen.

In the next chapter, we'll dive deeper into the stories hiding in your money vault and how these stories have shaped every financial decision you've made until now. But first, take a moment to sit with what you've learned here. What is your money trying to tell you?

KEY TAKEAWAYS:
- Money communicates through emotions, patterns, and physical sensations
- Your financial behaviors create patterns that reveal deeper truths
- Physical and emotional responses to money contain valuable messages
- Every financial decision tells a story about your beliefs and values

CHAPTER 2

The Stories in Your Vault

I'll never forget the sound of my lopsided air mattress wheezing against the bare floor of the tiny two-bedroom apartment I shared with a family of seven. Some nights, the gentle hiss of escaping air competed with the gnawing emptiness in my stomach for my attention. Those hungry nights—when sleep was my only meal—taught me lessons about money I'd never forget. They also led me to a decision that would change everything: I joined the Army.

The military offered stability I'd never known, and with that stability came a new hunger. Not for food this time, but for increased financial knowledge. I threw myself into adding to my financial knowledge bank every chance I got, and when I discovered how investing worked, it felt like uncovering a secret that had been kept from me my whole life. Money could grow by itself? The market could do the heavy lifting while I slept? This was revolutionary, and like many who discovered a life-changing truth, I wanted to share it with everyone I knew.

"You have to hear this," I told my battle buddy during one of our breaks. My eyes were bright with excitement as I explained the power of stocks and dividends. I'd brought charts, examples—everything I thought would make the opportunity as clear to her as it was to me.

She looked at me like I had two heads. "Girl, you are crazy to think I would ever put money in the stock market." Her voice carried the weight of absolute certainty. "The stock market is for certain people, and I am not certain people. I refuse to lose my money like my uncle did."

Her words stopped me cold. It wasn't just the rejection of the investment strategy—it was the story behind it. At that moment, I glimpsed the power of inherited money stories. Her uncle's loss wasn't just a financial event; it had become a family legend, a cautionary tale that now shaped her entire relationship with wealth building.

That conversation lived rent-free in my head for years. While I saw the market as a path to freedom, she saw it through the lens of her uncle's loss. It was the same financial tool but completely different stories. Her response made me realize that sharing financial knowledge wasn't enough—we all carry deeply personal stories about money that filter how we receive and act on that knowledge.

This insight transformed my approach to financial education and coaching. I learned to listen first to people's stories about money; the memories, beliefs, and family legacies that shape their financial decisions, because here's the truth I've discovered: Behind every money choice, there's a story. Behind every financial pattern, there's a narrative waiting to be understood.

Everyone has a money vault. Behind its heavy doors lie the stories that shape every financial decision you make—stories you might not even know you're carrying. These aren't just distant memories filed away in some dusty corner of your mind. They're active scripts running in the background of your financial life, influencing everything from how you negotiate your salary to whether you check your bank balance.

For some, it's the memory of watching parents argue about bills at the kitchen table, voices hushed but tension palpable. That story might now whisper, "Money causes conflict," whenever you need to have a financial discussion with your partner. For others, it's the shame of being the kid with the off-brand sneakers, a story that might drive you to overspend on your children today. Or perhaps it's the pride of watching a grandmother count her savings in church envelopes, teaching you the sacred value of every dollar—a story that gave you discipline but might also keep you from enjoying the wealth you've created.

These stories aren't just memories. They're the blueprint for your financial life, the invisible architecture that shapes every money decision you make. They determine whether you ask for that raise, how you feel about debt, whether you believe wealth is possible, and even how you define "enough."

Opening the Vault

Think of your money vault as a long-forgotten safety deposit box. You might not remember exactly what's inside, but its contents are precious—not because they're all valuable, but because they've been guiding your financial journey all along. Opening this vault requires courage because what you find inside might challenge everything you believe about your relationship with money.

When specific money patterns keep repeating in your life—perhaps you consistently under-save despite a good income, or you find yourself playing small in business—it's often because there's a story in your vault running the show. These patterns aren't random. They're the faithful execution of scripts you inherited or developed long ago.

Your inherited financial beliefs are particularly powerful because they were established during your most formative years. You absorbed them through what you were told about money and what you witnessed, felt, and experienced. Every raised eyebrow at a purchase, every celebration of a financial win, every whispered concern about bills—these moments wrote lines in your money story that still shape your decisions today.

The cost of keeping your vault locked is high. When we refuse to examine these stories, they continue to direct our financial lives from the shadows. That promotion you never applied for? The investment opportunity you talked yourself out of? The business you dream of but haven't started? Behind each of these might be a vault story whispering, "Not for you," "Too risky," or "You don't deserve it."

But here's the truth that can set your financial future free: These stories shaped your past, but they don't have to determine your future. Understanding what's in your vault isn't about assigning blame or dwelling in the past. It's about bringing awareness to the scripts running your financial life so you can consciously choose which ones still serve you.

Opening your vault is the first step toward financial transformation. It's about shining a light on the stories directing your financial decisions from the shadows. Some of what you find will be wisdom worth keeping—the resilience, resourcefulness, and values that can serve as a foundation for your financial future. Other stories you'll discover are wounds waiting to be healed—the limiting beliefs, fears, and patterns that have kept you playing small.

As we explore your money vault, remember that every story inside it once served a purpose. Whether it still serves you or not, each belief somehow tries to protect or guide you. The goal isn't to discard everything you find but to consciously choose which stories you'll carry forward and which ones you're ready to release.

Inherited Wisdom vs. Inherited Wounds

Every family has its money language, passed down through generations like a complex recipe with both nourishing ingredients and elements that no longer serve us. Your grandmother's meticulous saving habits might have preserved your family through hard times, teaching valuable lessons about financial resilience. Yet perhaps those same habits, born from scarcity, also transmit a deep fear of spending that now holds you back from necessary investments in your future.

Understanding your financial inheritance requires looking at both sides of this coin. That aunt who started her business showed you what's possible with an entrepreneurial spirit. But maybe your father's business failure left invisible scars that make you hesitate to take calculated risks. Both experiences are part of your money story and have shaped your financial DNA.

Generational money patterns run deep. They show up subtly: the slight tension in your shoulders when you check your account balance, the reflexive "I can't afford that" before you even look at the price, or the guilt following a luxury purchase. These aren't just personal quirks; they're echoes of your family's financial history, reverberating through time.

Consider Maria, whose immigrant parents worked three jobs to provide for their family. Their dedication taught her invaluable lessons about work ethic and resilience. However, it also embedded a belief that success only comes through grinding, sacrifice, and struggle. While their wisdom about hard work served her well, the wound of equating success with suffering kept her from following easier paths to prosperity.

The key to transformation lies in becoming a conscious inheritor of your financial legacy. This means developing the discernment to recognize which money lessons are wisdom and which are wounds:

Wisdom looks like:

> The resourcefulness that helped your family survive tough times
>
> The value of saving for important goals
>
> The importance of living below your means
>
> The pride in earning your own way

Wounds often manifest as:

> Chronic underearning despite your capabilities
>
> Difficulty receiving financial abundance
>
> Compulsive saving that prevents necessary spending
>
> Shame around wanting more than you had growing up

Breaking cycles that no longer serve you doesn't mean rejecting your family's entire financial legacy. It means honoring the resilience and wisdom of those who came before you while consciously choosing which patterns to carry forward. Your ancestors did the best they could with what they knew. Now, with greater awareness and resources, you can build upon their wisdom while healing their wounds.

This healing happens through acknowledgment, not abandonment. When you recognize that your father's constant money anxiety came from his own childhood experiences of scarcity, you can be compassionate to his struggles while choosing a different relationship with abundance for yourself. When you understand that your mother's dismissal of wealth was protective—a way to make peace with limitation—you can appreciate her coping mechanism while allowing yourself to desire more.

The process of separating wisdom from wounds requires gentle curiosity. Rather than judging past patterns as simply "good" or "bad," ask:

> What was this belief trying to protect?
>
> How did this pattern serve my family at the time?
>
> What deeper value or wisdom lies beneath this habit?
>
> Does this pattern still serve my highest good?

As you sort through your inheritance, remember that you're not just healing your relationship with money; you're helping to transform your family's financial legacy for generations to come. Every wound you heal, every limiting pattern you break, creates new possibilities not just for you but for all who follow.

Your task now is not to discard your financial inheritance wholesale but to become its conscious curator. Like a skilled gardener, you get to choose which seeds from your family's money garden to nurture and which patterns to lovingly release—back to the soil of the past.

The Stories We Carry

Every vault has stories that echo through decades, shaping our financial reality with their persistent whispers. These narratives aren't just thoughts but deeply embedded beliefs that influence every money decision. Research confirms the profound impact of these early money stories. According to the Federal Reserve Bank of St. Louis, our core financial habits are typically formed by age 7. Yet despite this powerful early conditioning, a 2023 T. Rowe Price study found that 69% of parents experience reluctance in talking to their kids about money. This silence allows inherited money patterns to continue unchallenged, passing from one generation to the next. Let's illuminate some of the most common stories and understand their profound impact on our financial lives.

"Money is hard to come by." This story often takes root when we witness struggle early in life. Perhaps you watched your parents work multiple jobs or heard constant conversations about how difficult it was to "make ends meet." While this narrative might have accurately described your past circumstances, it creates a self-fulfilling prophecy in the present. When we believe money is inherently difficult to obtain, we subconsciously create resistance to receiving it. We might overlook opportunities, undersell our services, or talk ourselves out of asking for raises—all because our story tells us it's supposed to be hard.

The impact of this belief extends beyond our earning potential. It affects how we handle money when we do receive it. Those carrying this story often grip too tightly to what they have, operating from a place of scarcity even when surrounded by abundance. Every financial decision becomes weighted with stress, and the natural flow of money—both in and out—feels blocked.

"Wealthy people are bad." This narrative often takes shape through childhood observations of class differences or absorbing societal messages about wealth and morality. Maybe you heard comments about "those rich people" in your community or internalized media portrayals of wealthy individuals as corrupt or unhappy. This view is particularly insidious because it creates an inner conflict; part of you wants financial success, while another part believes achieving it would make you a bad person.

When this story runs in the background, it can cause self-sabotage just as success comes within reach. You might find yourself making poor financial decisions, refusing opportunities, or subconsciously spending money to stay in your "good person" comfort zone. This perspective creates a false choice between being wealthy and being worthy.

"I have to work twice as hard." This story often emerges from experiences of marginalization or family messages about proving oneself in an unfair world. While it might have originated as a strategy for overcoming real obstacles, it can transform into a crushing burden that denies you the right to ease and efficiency in your financial life.

Those ascribing to this story often resist shortcuts, ignore opportunities for passive income, or feel guilty about "easy" money. Even when they achieve success, they might feel compelled to keep grinding, unable to enjoy the fruits of their labor. The story keeps them locked in a pattern of overwork, even when circumstances no longer require it.

"There's never enough." Perhaps the most common vault story, this narrative creates a persistent sense of lack—regardless of actual financial circumstances. It's the voice that whispers, "Save it for later," even when resources are abundant or triggers panic buying during sales because "we might run out." This story often originates from early experiences of scarcity or witnessing adults' anxiety about money.

The impact of this belief is far-reaching. It can drive compulsive earning, chronic overspending, or extreme frugality—all attempts to fill a perceived void that no amount of money seems to satisfy. People with this story might achieve significant wealth yet still feel poor or save compulsively while denying themselves basic pleasures.

These stories, while powerful, are not your destiny. Each one served a purpose in its time—offering protection, motivation, or a way to make sense of challenging circumstances. But recognizing them for what they are—stories, not immutable truths—is the first step toward choosing a new narrative.

Think of these stories like old maps. They might have helped you navigate past terrain but don't necessarily reflect your current landscape or where you want to go. The question isn't whether these stories are "true" or "false" but whether they still serve your highest good and support the financial future you want to create.

As you identify these stories in your vault, remember: You're not alone in carrying them. These narratives are often woven into the fabric of families, communities, and cultures. Recognizing them isn't about assigning blame; it's about reclaiming your power to write new stories that better serve your present and future.

Transformational Moment: The Vault Inventory

Now comes a pivotal moment in your journey: taking inventory of your own money vault. Find a quiet space where you won't be interrupted. You'll need your journal, something to write with, and the courage to look at your stories with honest, compassionate eyes. This inventory isn't about judgment; it's about discovery.

First Money Memories

Close your eyes. Return to your earliest money memory. Write down:

What happened?
How did it make you feel?
What did it teach you about money?

Family Money Messages

What three phrases about money did you hear most often growing up? Write them down exactly as you remember them, including who said them and how they affected you.

Your Current Money Patterns

Look at your financial life today. When do you feel most triggered around money? Note your automatic responses to financial situations:

What makes you anxious?

Where do you feel stuck?

What financial decisions do you tend to avoid?

Core Story Identification

Based on your reflections, identify the main story running your financial life. Complete this sentence: "The story I tell myself about money is..."

The Crossroads

Answer these two questions:

1. How has this story protected you?

2. What would be possible if you wrote a new story?

Take a moment to sit with what you've discovered. These insights are the first step toward conscious choice about the money stories you carry forward.

[Note: You can use this framework for deeper exploration in your own time, returning to specific memories or patterns that feel particularly significant.]

Unlocking the Patterns

Our vault stories don't stay locked away in the past; they actively choreograph our present-day money dance. Like an invisible script running in the background, these stories surface in the most mundane financial moments of our daily lives.

Consider the subtle ways your vault stories might be directing your financial choreography. That flutter of anxiety when you check your bank balance? It might be echoing the tension you felt watching your parents argue about money. The resistance you feel toward raising your prices? Perhaps it's channeling your grandmother's warnings about the dangers of wanting too much.

These stories reveal themselves in patterns so familiar we often mistake them for personality traits. What we consider being "bad with money" or "a natural saver" might actually be the faithful reproduction of inherited money stories.

The Past in Your Present

Your vault stories become your money reflexes. They show up in split-second decisions and gut reactions:

The immediate "no" to an investment opportunity before hearing the details.

The impulse to spend a bonus immediately "before it disappears."

The instinct to hide good financial news from family members.

The urge to self-sabotage just as success comes within reach.

Each of these reactions has roots in your money past, connecting to specific experiences or messages that shaped your financial beliefs.

Story Triggers

Certain situations reliably activate our vault stories, much like pressing play on an old recording. Learning to recognize these triggers is key to changing the pattern. Common trigger points include:

Opening bills or financial statements

Discussing money with partners or family

Making large purchases

Receiving unexpected money

Asking for payment or raising prices

Comparing yourself to peers' financial success

When triggered, we often go into autopilot, letting our old stories drive our decisions. The key is catching ourselves in that crucial moment between trigger and reaction. This pause—even if just for a breath—creates space for choice rather than compulsion.

Your Financial Defense System

We all develop sophisticated mechanisms to protect ourselves from financial pain or perceived threats. These defense mechanisms might have served us well once, but they often outlive their usefulness.

Think of the person who chronically overworks, always taking on extra projects despite healthy savings. Their defense mechanism—constant earning—might stem from a childhood story about financial security being forever fragile. Or consider someone who immediately spends any extra money, unconsciously ensuring they stay in their financial comfort zone because prosperity feels dangerous based on their vault stories.

Common defense patterns include:

Avoidance: Refusing to look at bank statements, delaying financial decisions, or procrastinating on money conversations.

Over-control: Micromanaging every penny, refusing to delegate financial tasks, or being unable to enjoy spending even when it is affordable.

Rebellion: Impulsive spending, rejecting practical financial advice, or deliberately choosing the opposite of what family members would do.

Perfectionism: Waiting for the "perfect" time to invest, needing to understand everything before taking action, or setting impossible financial standards.

These patterns aren't character flaws but protective adaptations to your money story. Understanding them with compassion is the first step toward choosing new responses.

The real power lies in recognizing these patterns as they emerge. When you notice yourself in a familiar financial reaction, pause and ask:

What story from my vault is playing right now?

What am I trying to protect myself from?

What would be possible if I responded differently?

This awareness creates a pivot point: a moment where you can choose whether to follow the old pattern or write a new story. You might still choose the familiar path sometimes, but it becomes a conscious choice rather than an unconscious compulsion.

Remember, these patterns developed for good reasons. They helped you navigate past financial waters. The question isn't whether they're "right" or "wrong," but whether they're still serving your highest good in the present moment. As you develop this awareness, you gain the power to respond rather than react, to choose rather than default, and to write new patterns that align with the financial future you're creating.

Rewriting the Narrative

Now that you've identified your vault stories, you stand at a powerful crossroads. This is the moment when awareness transforms into choice. Not every story in your vault needs to be discarded; some carry wisdom worth preserving. The key is consciously choosing which stories continue to serve your highest good and which ones you're ready to release.

Consider your vault stories like a family heirloom collection. Some pieces are treasures worth keeping—perhaps your father's lesson about saving for opportunities or your grandmother's wisdom about generous giving. Other pieces, like the belief that money corrupts or success requires suffering, may be ready for retirement. You get to be the curator of your financial narrative, thoughtfully selecting which stories to carry forward.

Creating new money beliefs isn't about positive thinking or affirmations alone. It's about aligning your financial story with your deepest truth. This means examining each inherited belief and asking: Does this support the life I'm creating? Does it reflect what I know to be true about abundance and possibility? Does it honor both my past and my future?

Building a stronger financial foundation begins with understanding that your intrinsic worth isn't determined by your net worth. Your new story might acknowledge past struggles while remaining open to future ease. It might honor your family's resilience while permitting you to succeed differently. Each conscious choice to respond, rather than react, helps lay another brick in this foundation.

Your next chapter is already waiting to be written. It starts with small edits to your daily money story—catching yourself when old patterns emerge and choosing a new response. It grows stronger each time you allow yourself to want more without guilt, to receive without shame, and to succeed without fear. This isn't about rejecting your past; it's about expanding what's possible for your future.

Wealth Wisdom Reflection:
1. What's the earliest money memory in your vault?
2. Which family money patterns do you want to keep?
3. What new money story are you ready to write?
4. How will future generations benefit from your story transformation?

The Porch Promise: A Little Girl Chooses a New Money Story

Perhaps no one embodies the power of rewriting your money story more profoundly than Oprah Winfrey. Born into poverty in rural Mississippi, her early vault stories were written in scarcity. She wore dresses made from potato sacks, lived without running water, and learned the sting of material lack early. Her childhood vault held stories that whispered, "This is all there is," and "This is what you deserve."

But even as a young girl, Oprah began to sense a different story was possible. "I remember standing on my grandmother's front porch in Mississippi at four years old," she once shared, "and thinking, 'My life will not be like this. My life will be better.'" That moment of clarity—that rejection of an inherited story of lack—became the first line in her new money narrative.

What makes Oprah's story so powerful isn't just her rise from poverty to billions. It's how she consciously refused to let her childhood money stories define her future. Where poverty could have taught her to hoard wealth, she became known for legendary generosity. Where scarcity could have made her fearful of loss, she took bold business risks. Where lack could have made her clutch tightly to every dollar, she created waves of abundance that lifted others.

Most remarkably, Oprah didn't just change her own money story; she made it her mission to help others rewrite theirs. Through her platform, she consistently challenged limiting beliefs about wealth and worth, especially for women and people of color. She demonstrated that your starting story doesn't have to be your ending story.

When asked about her relationship with money today, Oprah speaks not of fear or lack but of flow and purpose. She's transformed her vault stories from "there's never enough" to "there's more than enough to share." From "money is scarce" to "abundance is my birthright."

Her journey reminds us that every money story can be rewritten. Every vault can be transformed from a chamber of limitation to a treasury of possibility. Your current financial reality may reflect stories you inherited, but your future financial story? That's yours to write.

Your vault stories have shaped your journey until now, but they don't have to determine your future.

In the next chapter, we'll explore how your worth whispers beneath these stories, waiting to guide you toward a new financial reality. But first, take a moment to honor the stories that brought you here—both the ones you'll keep and the ones you're ready to release.

KEY TAKEAWAYS:
- Your money vault contains inherited beliefs and experiences
- Early financial experiences shape current money decisions
- Family patterns influence your relationship with wealth
- Understanding your stories is key to transformation

CHAPTER 3

When Worth Whispers

When I first started my coaching business, anything involving technology felt like trying to solve a Rubik's cube in the dark. A financial colleague referred me to Cora, describing her as "talented and extremely proficient." I didn't understand what she meant until I saw Cora's work firsthand.

Our first meeting was supposed to be a quick consultation about setting up my client management system. Instead, Cora transformed my entire digital presence in under an hour. Her fingers flew across the keyboard, elegantly solving problems I didn't even know I had. She created workflows that seemed to read my mind, designed layouts that perfectly captured my brand's essence, and implemented automation that made my previous systems look like they belonged in the Stone Age.

"This is... incredible," I said, watching my business transform before my eyes. "How long have you been doing this?"

"About three years," she replied, her voice lacking the confidence her skills demanded. She continued working, each click and keystroke demonstrating mastery that would have taken me months to even begin to understand.

"And what do you typically charge for this level of work?" I asked, already sensing her answer wouldn't match her value.

Cora's fingers froze above the keyboard. A flush crept up her neck as she named a figure so low it made my heart sink. Her rate was less than what I charged for thirty minutes of coaching, yet here she was, providing solutions that would generate value for my business for years to come.

"Why?" I asked softly.

She looked up, startled. "Why what?"

"Why are your rates so low when your work is so exceptional?"

The question seemed to catch her off guard, as if no one had ever challenged her pricing before. She stuttered, her professional demeanor cracking.

"I... I, I guess I was thinking if my prices were more affordable, people would hire me." Her voice grew smaller with each word. "There are so many others doing this kind of work... I just wanted to make sure I could compete."

"Cora," I said, turning away from the stunning updates she'd just created, "Let me ask you something. If I had to learn how to do what you've just done for me, how long do you think it would take?"

She considered this. "Well, depending on your technical background... maybe three to four months to learn the basics?"

"And would I be able to create something of this quality?"

A hint of pride finally crept into her voice. "Probably not without a lot more practice."

"So, you've just saved me months of learning time, created something far better than I could have managed on my own, and solved problems I didn't even know I had... and you think you need to be 'affordable' to compete?"

The number in your bank account isn't a measure of your worth. But your sense of worth is absolutely impacting what you allow into your bank account.

Think about it. When was the last time you:

Said yes to a price that felt too low?

Avoided asking for a raise you deserved?

Felt guilty about charging what you're worth?

Apologized for your rates?

Discounted your services before anyone asked?

That wasn't your bank account talking. That was your worth whispering.

The Worth-Wealth Connection

Most of us have been taught that wealth comes from a simple equation: skills plus opportunity equals income. Work harder, learn more, find the right chances, and the money will follow. But this equation is missing its most crucial variable: worth.

Your sense of worth isn't just one factor in your financial life; it's the foundation that determines how you use every other factor. It's the invisible force that shapes every financial decision you make. It sets the ceiling on any request and whispers limitations about what you deserve. It determines which opportunities you'll pursue and which you'll let pass by. It stands with you—or abandons you—in negotiations. Most importantly, it shapes how you present your value to the world, speaking either in confident declarations or hesitant whispers.

The impact of worth on wealth is measurable. PayScale's 2023 study found that women who consistently negotiate their salaries—a key indicator of worth confidence—earn $1 million more over their careers than those who don't. According to LinkedIn's 2023 Workforce Confidence Index, professionals who rate themselves as 'very confident' earn on average 28% more than those who express self-doubt.

Knowledge alone doesn't increase income. If it did, every well-educated professional would be wealthy. Skills don't guarantee higher earnings; if they did, every talented artisan would be prosperous. The missing link between capability and compensation isn't external at all. It's the internal permission slip you write yourself, signed with the ink of your self-worth.

The truth is, your worth operates like a thermostat for your wealth. You can push for higher earnings, but if your worth thermostat is set low, you'll unconsciously find ways to return to your comfort zone. You'll work with clients who undervalue you, accept less than you deserve, or self-sabotage just as success comes within reach. Until you adjust your worth thermostat, your financial temperature will always return to what feels familiar—even if what's familiar isn't what you truly desire.

Recognizing Worth Whispers

Worth whispers are subtle. They mask themselves as practicality, humility, or good business sense, like a familiar song playing so softly in the background you hardly notice it's there. These whispers shape your decisions without announcing their presence, but once you learn to recognize them, you'll hear them everywhere.

Consider the last time you discussed your rates or salary. Did you find yourself explaining, justifying, or apologizing for your prices? That's a worth whisper. When you present your services, do you lead with your credentials, hoping they'll prove your value? Another whisper. Each time you say "just" before stating your fee or add, "but I'm flexible" to the end of your price, your worth is whispering its doubt.

These whispers show up in countless ways throughout your day. You might find yourself over-delivering—far beyond what you promised—hoping to prove you deserve what you charged. Perhaps you hesitate to raise your rates even when you're fully booked, telling yourself the market isn't ready. You might notice yourself saying yes to projects that feel too small, convincing yourself it's good to stay humble.

The language of low self-worth has its own distinct dialect. It speaks in disclaimers: "I'm not an expert, but..."

It hedges with qualifiers: "This might not be worth much, but..."

It diminishes achievements: "I got lucky" or "Anyone could do this."

Listen closely to your professional vocabulary. Are you "just checking in" on proposals? Are you "wondering if maybe" you could discuss a raise? These verbal habits aren't just communication patterns—they're worth whispers made audible.

In your money decisions, these whispers become actions. You might find yourself extending payment terms you can't afford because you fear losing a client. You wait to invoice, telling yourself you're being considerate when you're really just avoiding claiming your value. You offer discounts at the first hint of hesitation or agree to scope creep without adjusting your fee. Each of these decisions carries a worth whisper within it.

The most insidious worth whispers often come disguised as virtue. "I want to be accessible," you might say, keeping your prices artificially low. "I don't do this for the money," you declare, as if being compensated fairly somehow diminishes your impact. "Others need it more," you tell yourself, stepping back from opportunities. These noble-sounding justifications often mask a deeper unwillingness to claim your full value.

Perhaps the loudest worth whisper of all is silence—the opportunities you don't pursue, the raises you don't request, the prices you don't quote. Every time you hold back from expressing your value, every client you don't approach because they seem "too big," every time you talk yourself out of applying for a position because you're "not quite ready," your worth is whispering its limitations.

But recognizing these whispers isn't about self-judgment. It's about awareness. Each whisper is an invitation to listen more deeply, to understand the stories you've internalized about your value. They're pointing to places where your worth wants to speak up—where it's ready to transform from a whisper into a declaration.

Start paying attention to these moments. Notice when you feel the urge to discount, apologize, or over-explain. Observe when you shy away from claiming your expertise or hesitate to name your value. These aren't character flaws or professional shortcomings; they're worth whispers asking for your attention. Once you can hear them clearly, you can begin to change their tone.

Transformational Moment: The Mirror Exercise

Find a quiet moment alone. You'll need a mirror, somewhere private where you won't be interrupted, and the courage to look yourself in the eyes. This exercise often brings up unexpected emotions. That's not only normal, it's part of the process.

Stand before your mirror. Take a deep breath. Let your shoulders relax. Now, look directly into your own eyes.

We're going to do something that might feel uncomfortable at first: You're going to state your value out loud to yourself. This means saying your rates or prices if you're a business owner. If you're employed, this means stating the salary you want to ask for. Whatever number represents your next level of worth-aligned income, that's what you'll declare.

Start with these words: "My rate is…" or "My salary requirement is…"

Say the number clearly, at full volume. Notice what happens in your body as you do. Do your eyes want to look away? Does your voice try to shrink? Does your throat tighten? Pay attention to any physical sensations: tension in your shoulders, a flutter in your stomach, an urge to cross your arms. These bodily responses are your worth whispers taking physical form.

Now, say it again. This time, add these words after your number: "…and I'm worth every penny."

Notice what that feels like.

Does it feel true?

Does it feel false?

Does something inside you want to argue with it?

These reactions are worth whispers becoming audible.

Try it a third time, but now, imagine you're stating this number to your ideal client or employer. Watch your face as you speak. Do you smile apologetically? Do you rush through the number? Do you feel an urge to justify or explain immediately? These are the habits that have been quietly shaping your worth story.

Stay with yourself for a moment. Look at the person in the mirror—the one who has worked so hard, learned so much, and overcome so many challenges. That person deserves to be valued fully. That person deserves to speak their worth at full volume.

Now, one final time, state your number. But this time, imagine you're speaking not just for yourself but for everyone who looks up to you. For those who will come after you. For those who need to see someone claim their full worth without apology. Let your voice carry all of that power.

What you just experienced—every flutter of doubt, every urge to look away, every impulse to explain or justify—were your worth whispers revealing themselves. But you also experienced something else: the power of looking directly at your worth and hearing your voice claim your value.

This mirror will always tell you the truth. Return to it whenever you need to practice speaking your worth at full volume. Use it before important negotiations. Stand before it when you're preparing to raise your rates. Let it witness your transformation from worth whispers to worth declarations.

Remember, discomfort with this exercise doesn't mean you're asking for too much—it means you're finally asking for enough. The mirror doesn't lie. If you can stand in your truth before it, you can stand in your worth anywhere.

The Anatomy of Worth

Your worth story didn't begin with you. Like a tree, your sense of worth has roots that reach deep into the soil of your past, drawing nourishment, or toxicity, from experiences that happened long before you set your first price or negotiated your first salary.

Understanding your worth foundation begins with recognizing that your earliest money experiences laid the first stones. Perhaps you grew up hearing, "We can't afford that," or "Money doesn't grow on trees." Maybe you watched a parent struggle to ask for what they deserved or observed the painful dance of financial shame. These experiences weren't just about money—they were your first lessons in worth.

Think of your worth foundation as layers of sediment, each experience depositing its own message: the praise you received for being "humble," the warnings about not getting "too big for your boots." The subtle implications that wanting more meant being greedy. These messages settled into your foundation, creating the bedrock upon which you would later build your relationship with money.

But within this foundation lie worth wounds: those moments when your value was questioned, dismissed, or denied; your creative work was devalued; when the promotion went to someone less qualified; or the client who haggled your price down until you felt almost ashamed to accept payment. These wounds aren't mere memories; they're active forces shaping your current money decisions.

Some worth wounds run deeper still. Perhaps you learned early in life that your value depended on your achievements or that asking for what you needed meant being "difficult." Maybe you internalized the message that certain people—people who look like you, sound like you, come from where you come from—shouldn't expect too much. These profound wounds don't just hurt; they become the lens through which you view your own value.

Your worth triggers are the modern-day echoes of these ancient wounds. They're the reason a simple price negotiation can suddenly feel loaded with emotion. They explain why certain clients or situations instantly activate your self-doubt or why specific money conversations send you straight into overcompensating or undercharging. These triggers aren't character flaws—they're your worth wounds.

Observe how your worth responds when someone questions your rates. Notice what happens inside when a client takes too long to reply to a proposal. Pay attention to the feelings that arise when someone with less experience charges more than you do. These moments of activation aren't random; they're your worth triggers revealing themselves.

But understanding your worth anatomy isn't about dwelling in old wounds. It's about developing worth resilience: the capacity to hold your value steady even when circumstances challenge it. Worth resilience grows from acknowledging your wounds while refusing to let them determine your future.

Building this resilience begins with recognition. When a worth trigger activates, name it: "This is my old story about not being enough." When a worth wound throbs, acknowledge it: "I see how this past hurt is shaping my present choice." This awareness itself becomes a form of healing.

Worth resilience also means creating new reference points for your value. You strengthen your worth foundation each time you maintain your rates, despite pressure to lower them. You build resilience every time you ask for what you deserve without apologizing. You heal old wounds when you choose to walk away from opportunities that require you to diminish your value.

Think of your worth like a muscle. It can be wounded, yes, but it can also be strengthened. It has memory, but it can learn new patterns. It may carry past scars, but these scars can become sources of wisdom and strength. Your worth anatomy isn't fixed; it's a living, growing thing capable of tremendous healing and expansion.

The question isn't whether you have worth wounds or triggers—we all do. The question is: Will you let them continue whispering limitations, or will you use them as stepping stones toward a more resilient sense of value? Understanding your worth anatomy is the first step in choosing your answer.

Worth Barriers

Every journey toward claiming your worth encounters resistance. Like ancient guardians protecting a sacred temple, these worth barriers rise just when you're ready to step into your next level of value. Understanding these barriers—and their antidotes—is crucial for your worth evolution.

"Who am I to charge that much?"

This whisper often disguises itself as humility, but beneath its modest exterior lies one of the most powerful worth barriers you'll face. It suggests that claiming your value is an act of arrogance and that staying small is somehow more virtuous than standing in your power.

The truth? Who are you not to charge that much? Your pricing isn't just about you; it's about the value you create, the transformation you deliver, and the difference you make. When you undercharge, you're not just diminishing your worth; you're diminishing the importance of your work in the world. Your clients aren't paying for your time; they're investing in the unique way you solve problems, the specific wisdom you've gained, and the particular magic that happens when they work with you.

"Others can do it better."

This barrier masquerades as reasonable self-assessment, but it's actually a myth about value requiring perfection. It whispers that you don't deserve to be well-compensated unless you're the absolute best. It suggests there's only room for one expert, leader, and voice.

Consider this: People don't hire the best; they hire the one they connect with, trust, and can access. Your clients choose you not because you're better than everyone else but because you're exactly who they need. Your unique combination of skills, perspective, and approach creates value in a way no one else can replicate. The existence of other experts doesn't diminish your worth—it simply proves there's an abundant need for what you offer.

"I need more credentials."

This barrier often feels productive—after all, what's wrong with wanting to improve? But beneath this, seemingly responsible, desire for more preparation often lies a deeper pattern of perpetual postponement. It's the voice that says you'll be worth more after the next certification, the next degree, the next training.

The reality is that while education has value, credentials don't create worth—impact does. Your worth isn't waiting for your next certification; it's already present in the results you help create, the problems you solve, and the transformations you facilitate. Your lived experience, your earned wisdom, your battle-tested insights—these are credentials that no institution can grant.

"I should be grateful for what I have."

Perhaps the most insidious barrier of all, this one weaponizes gratitude against growth. It implies that wanting more somehow negates appreciation for what you have and that ambition and gratitude can't coexist within the same heart.

Genuine gratitude doesn't require you to settle. You can be deeply thankful for where you are while honoring your call to grow. Gratitude and worth aren't opponents—they're allies. Being grateful for your current clients doesn't mean you can't raise your rates. Appreciating your current salary doesn't mean you can't ask for a raise. Evolution isn't ingratitude; it's how you honor the gifts you've been given.

These barriers don't appear randomly; they surface most strongly when you're on the verge of expanding or about to claim a new level of worth. They're not signs that you're doing something wrong—they're indicators that you're growing into a new dimension of your value.

The antidote to these barriers isn't to fight them or to shame yourself for having them. Instead, welcome them as familiar friends who are trying, in their misguided way, to protect you. Thank them for their concern. Then, gently remind them that you're ready to speak your worth at full volume.

Remember: These barriers arose from experiences that taught you to protect yourself by staying small. But you're not in those experiences any more. You've grown. You've evolved. You've proven your value countless times. The only question is: Are you ready to let your worth speak louder than your barriers?

Building Your Worth Muscle

Like any muscle, your worth grows stronger through consistent, intentional practice. This isn't about hollow affirmations or temporary confidence boosts. It's about developing the deep, lasting strength that comes from regularly choosing your worth over your familiar patterns of self-doubt.

Creating worth-based boundaries begins with a simple but profound shift: letting your worth, not your fear, set your limits. When a client asks for a rush job, your fear might whisper, "Say yes or lose them." But your worth speaks differently: "My time has value. Rush fees reflect that value." When someone wants to pick your brain over coffee, fear suggests you should be flattered. Worth calmly responds: "My expertise is valuable. Here's how we can work together formally."

These boundaries aren't walls—they're standards. They communicate not just what you will and won't do but also how you expect to be valued. You're strengthening your worth muscle each time you maintain a boundary, even when it feels uncomfortable. Each time you refuse to compromise your standards for short-term gain, you're building worth fitness.

Worth declarations are your daily strength training. Start small. Look in the mirror each morning and state your rates without apologizing. Send proposals without offering preemptive discounts. Remove qualifying language from your professional vocabulary; no more "just," "only," or "might." Replace "I think I can help" with "I know how to solve this." Each declaration builds your worth muscle's endurance.

First, practice worth declarations in low-stakes situations. Tell a friend about your recent accomplishments without minimizing them. Describe your expertise without self-deprecation. Share your rates with someone you trust, maintaining eye contact and steady breath. These seemingly simple exercises prepare you for bigger moments of worth declaration.

Developing price confidence is like progressive weight training; you build strength gradually, adding weight as you grow stronger. Begin by stating your current rates with conviction. Then, practice saying rates 10% higher. Then 20%. Notice the resistance point—where your voice wants to quaver, where doubt creeps in. That's exactly where your worth muscle needs strengthening.

Price confidence isn't about picking arbitrary numbers. It's about deeply understanding and owning the value you create. Track your results, document your client successes, and build a tangible record of your impact. Let this evidence inform your worth muscle's development. Your rates become statements of fact rather than leaps of faith.

Making decisions from worth means filtering every choice through one crucial question: "What would someone who truly values themselves do?" When an opportunity arises, worth asks: "Does this align with my value?" When challenges emerge, worth inquires: "How would my highest-worth self handle this?" These questions exercise your worth muscle in real-time situations.

This muscle memory becomes crucial in challenging moments: when a potential client balks at your rates, when a colleague questions your pricing, or when an opportunity tests your worth boundaries. In these moments, you don't need to consider holding your worth; your strengthened worth muscle responds automatically.

Remember that, like any muscle, your worth will experience fatigue. There will be days when maintaining boundaries feels exhausting, when worth declarations feel hollow, and when price confidence wavers. This isn't failure—it's part of the strengthening process. Just as physical muscles grow through stress and recovery, your worth muscle develops through challenge and renewal.

The key is consistency over intensity. Small, regular actions build more lasting strength than occasional grand gestures. Set a daily worth practice: one boundary maintained, one declaration made, one decision filtered through worth. Let these small choices accumulate into unshakeable worth strength.

Your worth muscle holds the power to transform not just your income but your entire relationship with value. Each time you exercise it—through boundaries, declarations, pricing, or decisions—you're building financial strength and developing the capacity to carry your full value into every area of your life.

The question isn't whether your worth muscle can grow stronger; it's whether you're ready to begin training. Start where you are, use what you have, and build from there. Your worth is ready for its workout.

Claiming Your Value

There comes a moment when understanding your worth must transform into claiming it. This isn't about what you deserve—it's about what you're ready to declare. The gap between knowing your value and claiming it is where most worth work stalls. Let's bridge that gap.

Setting worth-aligned prices begins with a fundamental truth: Your pricing isn't just about money—it's a statement of value. When you price from worth, you're not calculating what the market will bear or what your competitors charge. You're declaring what feels aligned with the transformation you create.

Start by getting quiet and asking yourself: "What would I charge if I fully trusted my value?" Notice the first number that arises. Now, notice the second number that comes after your initial fear response settles. This second number often reflects your true worth alignment. It might make you slightly uncomfortable. That's appropriate. Worth-aligned pricing should feel like a stretch, not a strain.

Consider this: Every time you set a price, you teach others how to value you. When you charge too little, you're not just undervaluing yourself; you're teaching others that your work isn't valuable. Your pricing becomes a form of leadership, showing others what's possible in your industry, particularly those coming after you who look to you as a model.

Having confident money conversations requires a new language—one free from the dialect of doubt. Remove phrases like "My regular rate is... but I can be flexible" or "Normally I charge... but for you..." These qualifiers don't serve connection; they serve fear. Instead, state your rates clearly, then create space. Let silence do the heavy lifting. Trust that your value doesn't require endless explanation.

Practice money conversations until they feel as natural as discussing the weather. Role-play with friends. Record yourself stating your rates. Notice where your voice shifts, where your energy wavers. These are the places where your worth still whispers. Keep practicing until your worth speaks clearly through every word.

Making unapologetic asks grows from the understanding that asking for what you're worth isn't an imposition—it's an invitation. When you ask for a raise, pitch a high-ticket offer, or name a significant fee, you invite others to participate in a fair exchange of value. You're not taking something from them; you're offering them something of worth.

The art of the unapologetic ask lies in your ability to separate the ask from the answer. Your worth isn't determined by whether someone says "yes" or "no". Make the ask clean and clear, unburdened by your attachment to the outcome. Your job is to ask for something aligned with your worth. Their job is to decide if it's right for them.

Standing firm in your value is where your worth practice faces its greatest tests. When a potential client pushes back on your rates, a colleague questions your pricing, and an opportunity asks you to compromise your worth standards, these moments reveal the strength of your worth foundation.

Remember: Standing firm doesn't mean being rigid. You can be flexible in how you package your offers while remaining solid in your value. You can negotiate terms while maintaining your worth. You can be kind and accommodating without compromising your standards.

Develop phrases that help you stand firm and gracefully:

"I understand this investment might not be right for you at this time."

"My pricing reflects the value and results I consistently deliver."

"I know I can create significant value at this level of investment."

"I've carefully set my rates to reflect the transformation I provide."

When standing firm feels challenging, remember this: Your worth isn't just about you. Every time you hold your value steady, you create ripples that affect everyone around you. You show others what's possible. You give permission for others to value themselves more fully. Your worth becomes a beacon.

The ultimate test of claiming your value isn't in the big moments—it's in the small, daily choices. It's declining opportunities that require you to shrink, sending proposals without preemptive discounts, introducing yourself with full confidence in your expertise, and letting your worth speak at full volume through every interaction.

Your value isn't something you need to create—it already exists. Claiming it isn't about becoming worthy; it's about aligning your actions with the worth you already possess. The question isn't whether you have value to claim. The question is: Are you ready to let your worth speak its whole truth through you?

Wealth Wisdom Reflection:

1. Where in your life are you accepting less than you're worth?
2. What would change if you fully believed in your value?

3. How might claiming your worth impact future generations?

4. What's the cost of staying small?

The Price of Recognition

It was time for the conversation to change. Watching Cora undervalue her extraordinary talents wasn't just about business anymore—it was about worth recognition. As someone dedicated to helping others step into their power, I couldn't let her continue dimming her light under the guise of being "affordable."

"Would you be open to exploring something with me?" I asked as she put the finishing touches on my website. She nodded, still focused on perfecting a detail most people wouldn't even notice—exactly the kind of dedication her current rates didn't reflect.

"I'm all for providing value and paying for it," I began, "but right now, this isn't a fair exchange. You're delivering Mercedes quality at bicycle prices."

Cora looked up, her expression a mix of surprise and discomfort. "But my clients seem happy with my rates..."

"Of course they're happy—they're getting an extraordinary deal. But happy clients don't always mean healthy business. What if your current pricing is actually doing them a disservice?"

She tilted her head, confused. "How could saving my clients money be a disservice?"

"Because when you severely undercharge, you teach people to undervalue not just your work, but your entire industry. You make it harder for everyone to charge their worth, including yourself. Plus, you limit your ability to invest in tools, training, and support that could help you serve even better."

I could see the wheels turning in her mind. Like many talented people, Cora hadn't realized that her rapid execution masked years of skill development.

She'd internalized the myth that if something came easily to her, it couldn't be that valuable—even though her ease was precisely what made her exceptional.

We spent the next hour in an impromptu coaching session, unpacking her worth whispers. We discovered that her father's business had failed during the recession, leaving her with a deep fear of "charging too much and losing everything." Her first client had haggled her prices down severely and she'd used that deeply discounted rate as her baseline ever since.

"But what if," I suggested, "your pricing isn't just about you? What if claiming your worth could actually inspire your clients to claim theirs?"

Something shifted in her expression—a recognition of what her worth journey could impact beyond her own bank account. We worked together to craft new packages and pricing that reflected her true value. Her hands shook as she typed the new numbers, but her spine straightened with each digit.

Three months later, an email arrived in my inbox:

"I have to share something with you. Remember how terrified I was to raise my prices? How convinced I was that no one would pay them? Well, I just ran my quarterly numbers. Since our conversation, my business is up 38%. But here's what really surprised me—I'm signing MORE clients, not fewer.

The most amazing part? They're better clients. They implement fully. They respect my time. They refer others. One client even told me, 'Your prices made me trust you more—I knew you had to be good to charge that much.'

But the real transformation isn't in my bank account (though that's pretty great!). It's in how I show up. I'm no longer rushing to prove my worth through endless extra work. I'm not apologizing for my rates. I'm actually sleeping at night instead of worrying about taking on every possible client to make ends meet.

Last week, a new tech VA in my network asked me for pricing advice. I found myself telling her exactly what you told me—that her worth wasn't determined by her fear but by her value. The worth whispers are still there sometimes, but now I know how to respond when they start.

Thank you for helping me see what I couldn't see for myself. My worth isn't just speaking anymore—it's singing."

Your worth isn't something you need to earn or prove—it's something you need to claim. As your worth whispers become worth declarations, you'll find yourself making different choices, setting different boundaries, and creating different financial results. In the next chapter, we'll explore how to trust these new worth-aligned decisions, but first, take a moment to hear what your worth is whispering right now. What is it asking you to claim?

KEY TAKEAWAYS:
- Your sense of worth directly impacts your wealth
- Worth whispers guide financial decisions
- Self-worth influences income and financial boundaries
- Worth patterns affect all money interactions

PART 2: ANSWERING THE CALL

CHAPTER 4

Opening Your Money Vault

It was a cold winter morning, and until I turned on my computer, I had no idea how much colder it was about to get. As I logged into my investment account, it felt like all the walls and windows had disappeared, exposing me to the bitter January air. Blood drained from my face as I watched my nest egg—my carefully tended financial future—flash a 60% loss.

Six months earlier, this scenario would have seemed impossible. I had been steadily building my wealth, following a conservative but effective strategy that had served me well.

"How is your investment portfolio looking, Jae?" my friend Vanessa asked during one of our monthly lunch meetups. "Oh, girl, it's looking really good," I beamed, my chest swelling with pride. Would you believe I've doubled my portfolio in the past three years?"

"That's good," Vanessa replied, but there was something in her tone—a hint of knowing superiority that should have been my first warning sign. "But guess what? We've been playing it too safe and leaving money on the table all this time." She pulled up charts and spreadsheets on her tablet, her manicured finger tracing the dramatic upward trajectories. "Instead of waiting three or more years to double our portfolio, we can do it in six months to a year!"

The strategy seemed revolutionary—a carefully orchestrated dance of options trading and leveraged positions that promised to accelerate wealth building beyond anything I'd imagined possible. Intrigued yet cautious, I found myself drawn into a world of investment webinars and exclusive group calls with their celebrated "guru."

Looking back, I can pinpoint the exact moment my gut screamed "No." It was during one of those late-night calls when the guru casually alluded to the "gazillions" he'd made in just a few short years. Something in his practiced confidence, the too-smooth way he deflected specific questions about risk management, set off alarm bells in my stomach but I couldn't articulate why. I couldn't point to any specific red flag that would justify turning down such a "proven" strategy.

The Army had taught me "If it ain't broke, don't fix it"—a lesson that had served me well in both military service and civilian life. But I pushed that wisdom aside, seduced by the possibility of making up for my late start in investing. "This could be a way to catch up," I convinced myself, drowning out my inner knowing with spreadsheets and calculations.

Have you ever had that feeling in your gut about a financial decision—that quiet knowledge that something wasn't quite right—but ignored it because it didn't seem "logical"? Perhaps it was that investment opportunity that looked perfect on paper but made your stomach clench. Or maybe it was that "can't-miss" business partnership that had impressive credentials but left you feeling inexplicably uneasy. We've all been there, standing at the crossroads of intuition and conventional wisdom, while our inner voice tries desperately to be heard.

How many times has that inner wisdom tried to guide you, only to be drowned out by the cacophony of external voices? There's the financial expert on television confidently predicting market trends, your well-meaning family members sharing stories of what worked for them, and an endless stream of social media "gurus" promising foolproof formulas for wealth. Traditional financial rules echo in your mind, reminding you what you "should" do, while other people's success stories tempt you to follow their path instead of your own.

In these moments, your authentic financial wisdom often gets buried under an avalanche of outside opinions and conventional thinking. The expert's credentials seem more trustworthy than your gut feeling. Your family's concerned advice weighs heavier than your innate knowledge. Those impressive success stories on social media appear more reliable than your personal intuition about what's right for you.

But what if everything you've been taught about financial decision-making has overlooked your most valuable asset—your own intuitive wisdom? What if your deepest financial wisdom isn't hidden in a spreadsheet or waiting to be discovered in a YouTube video but has been within you all along, quietly guiding you toward your truest path to prosperity?

The truth is, your inner understanding of money matters. That subtle feeling that makes you hesitate before signing a contract, that unexpected surge of excitement when considering a new investment, that persistent whisper suggesting a different approach—these aren't random feelings to be dismissed. They're expressions of your innate financial wisdom, shaped by your unique experiences, values, and knowledge of money.

This wisdom doesn't reject logic or ignore practical considerations. Instead, it integrates them with something deeper—your personal truth about what will truly serve your financial well-being. It's knowledge that goes beyond spreadsheets and statistics, incorporating your whole life experience and deepest understanding of what prosperity means for you.

The Wisdom Within

Financial intuition isn't some mystical force or random gut feeling; it's the culmination of your lived experience, emotional intelligence, and subconscious pattern recognition working in harmony. When you walk into a room of people, you instantly pick up on the energy and dynamics without consciously analyzing every detail. Your financial intuition works the same way, processing thousands of subtle cues and patterns that your conscious mind might miss in a spreadsheet or profit and loss statement.

Understanding this innate wisdom begins with recognizing its voice. Sometimes, it arrives as a physical sensation: a lightness in your chest when considering an investment that aligns with your values or a heaviness in your stomach when reviewing a contract that contains hidden pitfalls. Other times, it speaks through sudden clarity or persistent thoughts that won't let go, like that nagging feeling about diversifying your portfolio before a market downturn.

But here's where many of us get stuck: How do we distinguish between genuine financial wisdom and fear-based thinking? Fear speaks the language of scarcity, limitation, and worst-case scenarios. It's rooted in past traumas or future anxieties, often triggering a fight-or-flight response that clouds judgment. Wisdom, on the other hand, speaks with quiet confidence. It doesn't need to shout or catastrophize. It offers clear direction without the emotional charge of panic or desperation.

True power emerges when you make decisions that are aligned with both your intuitive wisdom and your conscious understanding. These aligned choices feel different; there's a sense of rightness that goes beyond just the numbers making sense. Think about times you've made decisions that looked perfect on paper but felt wrong beneath the surface. Perhaps you took that high-paying job that drained your spirit or invested in a "sure thing" that your gut warned you against. These moments of misalignment often teach us the most about trusting our deeper sense of knowing.

This brings us to an uncomfortable truth: Purely "logical" financial choices sometimes fail spectacularly. Why? Because traditional financial logic often operates on oversimplified assumptions about human behavior and marketplace dynamics. It can't fully account for the complex interplay of relationships, timing, and real-world complications that your intuition processes naturally. Consider the countless "foolproof" investment strategies that falter during black swan events or the meticulously planned business ventures that collapse due to unmeasurable human factors.

Your financial intuition integrates logic with a deeper understanding of your personal circumstances, values, and goals. It knows that the "mathematically optimal" choice isn't always the right one for your life context. It recognizes opportunities that spreadsheets miss and sees warning signs that algorithms can't detect. This isn't about abandoning rational analysis; it's about combining it with your innate wisdom to make decisions that serve your whole life, not just your bank account.

Think of your financial intuition as a skilled translator, helping you interpret the language of money through the lens of your authentic self. When you learn to trust and refine this internal guidance system, you'll find yourself making choices that aren't just financially sound, but also deeply aligned with who you are and what you truly want to create in the world.

Listening Levels

Learning to hear your financial wisdom requires understanding the different layers of "noise" that influence your money decisions. Like tuning a radio to find the clearest signal, you must learn to distinguish between various levels of financial input, each carrying its own frequency and significance.

At the most surface level, we encounter a constant barrage of external opinions. These are the voices that surround us daily: financial news headlines screaming about market shifts, colleagues sharing hot stock tips, and social media influencers promoting their latest wealth-building strategies. This surface noise is often the loudest and most insistent, demanding immediate attention and action. It's the cryptocurrency enthusiast insisting you'll miss out on the next big surge or the real estate guru claiming there's never been a better time to buy. While these voices might occasionally offer valuable insights, their volume often drowns out deeper wisdom.

Beneath this external chaos lies a more personal layer—mental chatter born from learned beliefs about money. These are the internal voices shaped by your upbringing, culture, and experience. Perhaps you hear your parents' warnings about financial security, replaying their Depression-era fears about saving every penny. Maybe you carry your community's beliefs about what constitutes "responsible" financial behavior or society's messages about what success should look like. This mental chatter often masquerades as wisdom, but it's really a collection of inherited beliefs that may or may not serve your authentic path.

Diving deeper, we encounter emotional signals—those gut feelings and instinctive responses to financial situations. Your heart races when considering a major investment, your shoulders tense during budget discussions, and your energy lifts when exploring a new business opportunity. These emotional signals aren't random; they're your body's way of processing complex financial information through the lens of your lived experience. While not all emotional responses should drive financial decisions, these signals often contain valuable information worth examining.

At the deepest level resides your true financial intuition—what we might call deep wisdom. This is the quiet, steady knowledge that emerges when other layers fall silent. Unlike the urgency of surface noise or the anxiety of mental chatter, this wisdom speaks with remarkable clarity and peace. It's the calm certainty you feel when making a decision that aligns with your authentic path, even if it defies conventional advice. This is the wisdom that knows when to take calculated risks, when to exercise patience, when to pursue opportunity, and when to practice restraint.

Learning to distinguish between these levels takes practice and presence. It requires creating space between financial stimuli and your response—a pause where you can ask yourself, "Which level is speaking right now?" Are you reacting to the latest market headlines? Responding to inherited beliefs about money? Following emotional impulses? Connecting with your deeper wisdom?

Consider a moment when you faced a significant financial decision. Perhaps it was changing careers, investing in your education, or starting a business. Surface noise might have bombarded you with opinions about the "smart" choice. Mental chatter might have recited all the reasons to play it safe. Emotional signals might have fluctuated between excitement and fear. But beneath it all, what was your deep wisdom saying? What did you know, on the most fundamental level, about the right path forward?

The key to accessing this deepest layer of financial wisdom lies not in silencing the other levels entirely—they all serve their purpose—but in developing the discernment to recognize which voice is speaking and give appropriate weight to each. Think of it as developing your financial intuition's perfect pitch, allowing you to tune out the distracting frequencies and zero in on the clear signal of your authentic knowing.

Transformational Moment: The Quiet Money Meditation

Find a quiet space where you won't be interrupted for the next fifteen minutes. This meditation is designed to help you access your deeper financial wisdom regarding a specific decision you're currently facing. Take a moment to bring that decision to mind; hold it gently in your awareness without trying to solve it.

Begin by settling into a comfortable position, either seated or lying down. Let your body relax into its natural weight, releasing any tension you're holding about money or this particular decision. Take three deep breaths, allowing each exhale to carry away some of the mental static surrounding your financial thoughts.

Now, imagine you're descending a beautiful staircase. With each step down, you're moving deeper beneath the surface of your everyday money thoughts. The voices of experts, the opinions of others, and the noise of the financial world all begin to fade with each step you take. Ten steps down... nine... eight... Notice how the mental chatter begins to quiet... seven... six... five... Feel yourself moving beneath the layer of learned beliefs about money... four... three... Sink below the surface of emotional reactions... two... one.

At the bottom of the staircase, you find yourself in a serene space—your personal wisdom room. This is where your deepest financial knowledge resides. The air here is clear and still. Notice how it feels to be in this space, free from external pressures and expectations about your decision.

In the center of this room is a comfortable seat—your wisdom seat. As you settle into it, feel how it completely supports you. This is where you can access your deepest knowledge of money. Bring your financial decision into this space, holding it like a gentle question in your open hands.

Rather than trying to figure out the answer, simply observe what emerges in this quiet space. What sensations arise in your body when you hold this decision in your awareness? Perhaps there's a feeling of expansion or contraction, warmth or coolness, heaviness or lightness. These subtle physical cues are often the first language of intuition.

Now, imagine your future self who has already made this decision wisely. They sit across from you, emanating a sense of peace and clarity. What would they want you to know about this choice? What wisdom do they carry that you're ready to access now? Let yourself receive any insights, images, or knowing that arrives, even if it seems unexpected or doesn't immediately make logical sense.

If you notice yourself starting to analyze or problem-solve, gently return to the sensation of sitting in your wisdom seat. Remember, you're not here to figure anything out, only to listen. What does your deepest wisdom want you to know about this decision? What becomes clear when you listen from this quiet place?

As insights emerge, let them settle into your awareness like soft rain into fertile soil. There's no need to grasp or hold onto them tightly. Your wisdom isn't going anywhere—it's always accessible when you create the space to listen.

Before you prepare to leave your wisdom room, take a moment to notice if there's anything else your intuition wants you to know about this decision. Sometimes, the quietest messages carry the most significance. Receive whatever final insights arise.

Now, imagine your wisdom seat dissolving into a pure golden light that fills your entire being. This light represents your innate capacity for clear financial intuition. It goes with you wherever you go and is available whenever you need to access it. As you prepare to ascend the staircase, know that you can return to this space anytime you need to connect with your deeper financial wisdom.

Slowly count yourself back up the stairs... one... two... three... Bring with you any insights or clarity you received... four... five... six... Let your awareness expand gently... seven... eight... nine... Gradually return to the present moment... ten.

Take a few moments to transition back, perhaps stretching gently or taking a deep breath. Before you open your eyes, place one hand over your heart and one over your belly, acknowledging these centers of intuitive wisdom in your body. When you're ready, open your eyes and take a moment to note any insights about your decision that emerged during this meditation.

Remember, you can return to this quiet space anytime you need to access your deeper financial knowledge. Sometimes, the most powerful guidance comes not from seeking more information but from creating the space to hear the wisdom that's already within you.

Developing Your Money Intuition

Developing your financial intuition requires intention, practice, and patience, just like any skill worth mastering. Think of it as cultivating a relationship with your inner financial advisor—one who knows your complete story and has only your best interests at heart. This development isn't about abandoning practical financial knowledge but rather about integrating it with your deeper wisdom to create a more holistic approach to money decisions.

Creating quiet space for financial clarity begins with establishing regular periods of financial reflection. This isn't about poring over spreadsheets or checking your credit obsessively. Instead, it's about creating sacred pauses in your day where you can step back from the noise of financial markets, social media, and other people's opinions. Perhaps it's fifteen minutes each morning before you check your phone or a quiet hour each weekend dedicated to connecting with your money energy. During these times, simply sit with your financial life: your hopes, concerns, and current decisions—without trying to solve or fix anything.

The key is consistency rather than duration. Even five minutes of focused attention can help you tune into your financial frequency. You might start by simply noting how different financial situations feel in your body. Does thinking about your savings create tension or ease? How does your energy shift when considering different investment opportunities? These physical sensations are often your intuition's first language, speaking through the wisdom of your body before your mind has time to analyze.

Building trust in your decisions requires keeping a wisdom journal: a record of times when you followed (or ignored) your financial intuition. Start documenting the subtle signs that preceded important money choices. Perhaps you felt unusually peaceful about a major purchase that others questioned, and it turned out to be a wise investment. Or maybe you ignored that persistent unease about a business partnership, only to learn valuable lessons when it unraveled. These experiences aren't failures or successes; they're data points helping you calibrate your intuitive compass.

This trust-building process also involves learning to distinguish between fear-based reactions and genuine intuitive guidance. Fear often shows up as rushed, panicked energy pushing you to act immediately. It speaks in absolutes and catastrophizes outcomes. Intuition, by contrast, tends to arrive with a sense of calm clarity, even when it's guiding you toward challenging decisions. It offers direction without attachment to specific outcomes.

Recognizing wisdom signals requires developing your personal intuitive dictionary. Your financial intuition might communicate through physical sensations, emotional shifts, recurring thoughts, or symbolic dreams. Some people experience their intuition as a subtle knowing in their solar plexus, while others receive clear mental images or unexplainable urges to take specific actions. Start noticing your personal patterns. When have your strongest intuitive hits come through? What were the circumstances? How did the message arrive?

Pay particular attention to what I call "wisdom whispers"—those subtle nudges that seem to arrive out of nowhere. Perhaps you suddenly think of diversifying your investments weeks before a market downturn, or you feel inexplicably drawn to learn about a new industry that later provides unexpected opportunities. These whispers often seem illogical in the moment but reveal their wisdom over time.

Strengthening your intuitive muscle happens through regular exercise, just like building physical strength. Start with small decisions where the stakes are lower. Before checking your account balance, pause and tune into what you think you'll find. Before opening a financial email, notice your intuitive sense about its contents. These micro-moments of intuitive practice build your confidence in accessing your inner awareness.

Challenge yourself to wait before making financial decisions, creating space between the impulse to act and the action itself. In this pause, notice what additional information or insights emerge. Sometimes, your initial intuitive hit will be confirmed; other times, waiting reveals deeper wisdom that wasn't immediately apparent.

Remember that developing your money intuition isn't about achieving perfect predictions or never making mistakes. It's about establishing a more nuanced and personal relationship with money that honors both practical wisdom and inner knowledge. Your intuition might guide you toward choices that seem counterintuitive to others yet they align perfectly with your authentic path to prosperity.

The goal is to develop a balanced approach where your analytical mind and intuitive wisdom work in partnership. Think of it as having both a skilled accountant and a wise sage on your personal financial board of directors. The accountant brings vital expertise about numbers and regulations, while the sage offers deeper insight about alignment and timing. Together, they help you navigate your financial journey with both practical savvy and soul-level wisdom.

Practical Intuition

While developing your financial intuition might sound ethereal or abstract, its real power emerges in the practical, everyday moments of your money life. This is where theory meets practice, where your inner wisdom guides not just the big decisions but the daily choices that shape your financial reality.

Using wisdom in daily money choices begins with bringing mindful awareness to your regular financial interactions. Consider how you engage with money in its most basic forms: paying bills, making purchases, and receiving income. Each of these moments offers an opportunity to practice accessing your intuitive wisdom. Before automatically paying a bill, pause to notice how this expense feels in your body. Does it create tension or feel like a natural exchange of energy? When making a purchase, check in with your intuition, beyond the surface desire or need. Is this transaction aligned with your deeper values and goals?

These daily choices might seem small, but they create the foundation of your financial life. Perhaps you're at the grocery store, deciding between organic and conventional produce. Instead of making this choice purely based on price or nutrition labels, take a moment to consult your inner wisdom. What's true for you in this moment? Maybe your intuition guides you to invest in certain organic items while choosing conventional for others, creating a balanced approach that honors both your health and your budget.

Or, consider your regular money management routines. Rather than checking your accounts on autopilot, create a ritual around this practice. Before logging in, take three conscious breaths and set an intention to receive whatever wisdom your numbers have to share. You might discover patterns you hadn't noticed before or receive unexpected insights about your spending and saving habits.

Balancing heart and head in financial decisions is not about choosing one over the other but rather, it's about creating a partnership between your emotional intelligence and your rational mind. Think of your heart as the compass that points toward your true financial north, while your head serves as the GPS calculating the most effective route to get there. Both are essential for successful navigation.

This balance becomes particularly crucial in investment decisions. While traditional financial advice focuses heavily on numbers and market analysis, your intuitive wisdom might offer equally valuable insights about timing, alignment, and long-term potential. Perhaps a particular investment looks perfect on paper, but something in your gut says, "Not yet." Or maybe an opportunity appears that doesn't fit conventional wisdom but strongly resonates with your inner knowledge about future trends.

Making confident decisions emerges from this integration of inner wisdom and outer knowledge. True confidence isn't about being certain of outcomes; it's about trusting your ability to make choices aligned with your complete financial intelligence. This kind of confidence has a different quality than mere bravado or wishful thinking. It carries a quiet sureness, an inner knowing that even if things don't work out as planned, you're making choices true to your wisdom.

This confidence grows as you develop a track record of listening to, and acting on, your intuitive hits. Keep a "wisdom log" of decisions made from this integrated place. Notice not just the outcomes but the quality of your experience along the way. Decisions made from genuine intuitive wisdom often feel different, even as they unfold, regardless of the final results.

Navigating conflicting advice becomes easier when you've developed a strong connection to your innate wisdom. In today's world, financial advice is abundant and often contradictory. One expert recommends aggressive investment in emerging markets, while another suggests conservative bonds. Your family might pressure you to buy property while your friends advocate staying liquid and mobile.

Rather than becoming paralyzed by these competing viewpoints, let your intuition serve as your primary filter. This doesn't mean ignoring external advice; instead, notice how different recommendations land in your body and align with your inner knowing. Some advice will resonate deeply, feeling like confirmation of what you already knew. Other guidance, though logical, might create internal discord.

Develop the practice of taking all advice on a "wisdom walk" by literally walking with a piece of guidance in mind while noticing how it feels in your body and spirit. Does it create expansion or contraction? Does it energize you or drain you? These physical and energetic responses are valuable data from your intuitive wisdom.

When facing particularly complex decisions with multiple sources of conflicting advice, create a wisdom council in your imagination. Picture yourself sitting in a circle with your various advisors, both external experts and your inner sense of knowing. Let each voice speak its truth, including your intuition. This practice often reveals ways to integrate different perspectives into a solution that honors practical wisdom and inner guidance.

Remember that your intuition becomes most practical when you treat it as a respected advisor rather than an infallible oracle. Like any trusted consultant, it provides valuable input to be considered alongside other sources of information. The key is learning to weigh this input appropriately, giving your inner wisdom the attention it deserves while remaining grounded in practical realities.

Regular practice lets you discover that practical intuition isn't about choosing between being spiritual or strategic with your money. It's about bringing your full, subtle, and practical wisdom to every financial choice you make. This integration leads to decisions that make sense on paper and feel deeply right in your body and spirit.

Trusting The Journey

The path to developing financial wisdom isn't linear. Like any journey of deep growth, it unfolds in spirals, sometimes bringing you back to familiar territories with new understanding, other times launching you into completely uncharted waters. Learning to trust this journey is perhaps the most crucial skill you'll develop in your relationship with money.

Building decision confidence doesn't happen overnight. It's cultivated through consistent practice and reflection. Think of it like developing any new skill; each decision is an opportunity to strengthen your wisdom muscle. Start by noticing how different types of financial choices feel in your body. A decision made from true confidence has a distinctive signature: a sense of calm certainty, even in the face of others' doubt or external challenges.

This isn't the bold confidence of someone who hasn't considered the risks, nor the false bravado of pushing aside legitimate concerns. Instead, it's a grounded knowledge that emerges from having developed a trustworthy relationship with your inner wisdom. You might still feel nervous about outcomes, but beneath that surface anxiety lies a steady trust in your ability to navigate whatever unfolds.

Consider keeping a "Confidence Chronicle": a regular record of your financial decisions and the various forms of wisdom that informed them. Note not just what you chose but how you arrived at each decision. What role did your intuition play? How did you integrate practical considerations? What were the subtle signs that guided you? Over time, patterns will emerge, helping you recognize your personal indicators of aligned decisions.

Many people struggle most with handling outcome uncertainty in their financial journey. Our culture's obsession with guaranteed results and predictable returns can make it challenging to trust decisions without clear assurances. Yet some of the most significant opportunities in life arrive without warranties or money-back guarantees.

The key lies in shifting your focus from controlling outcomes to trusting your process. When you've made a decision from a place of integrated wisdom—combining your intuition with practical due diligence—you can release the need to know exactly how things will unfold. This doesn't mean being passive or careless; rather, it means maintaining a dynamic balance between taking conscious action and allowing space for unexpected developments.

Think of uncertainty as the space where magic can enter. Just as nature requires both structure and flexibility to create new life, your financial journey needs both solid planning and room for surprise. Some of your most profitable ventures or wisest financial moves might arrive through unexpected channels, looking nothing like what you initially imagined.

Learning from every choice becomes possible when you view your financial journey as a continuous feedback loop rather than a series of successes and failures. Regardless of its outcome, each decision offers rich information about your relationship with money, your decision-making process, and the alignment between your inner wisdom and outer actions.

Even choices that don't yield the desired results can be invaluable teachers. Perhaps you ignored a subtle warning from your intuition and later understood why it was flagging concern. Or maybe you followed your inner guidance despite external criticism and discovered new strengths in standing firm with your intuition. These experiences become reference points for future decisions, gradually building your wisdom library.

Develop the practice of conducting gentle "Wisdom Reviews" after significant financial choices. Rather than judging outcomes as good or bad, explore questions like: What guidance did I receive? How did I respond? What can I learn about my decision-making process? What wisdom am I gaining that might serve future choices?

Creating wisdom patterns emerges naturally as you pay attention to how your intuition communicates and how different types of decisions unfold. You might notice that your most aligned financial choices share certain characteristics: perhaps a particular kind of clarity, a specific physical sensation, or a distinctive quality of knowing. These patterns become touchstones for future decisions.

Start documenting what I call your "Wisdom Signatures," the unique ways your intuition speaks to you about money. Perhaps you always get a specific type of dream before important financial shifts. Maybe your body offers clear signals about timing: a sensation of expansion when it's time to move forward or a feeling of contraction when it's wise to wait. These patterns are highly personal; what serves as a wisdom signal for one person might mean something entirely different for another.

Remember that building trust in your financial journey isn't about eliminating uncertainty or guaranteeing specific outcomes. It's about developing confidence in your ability to navigate whatever arises, knowing that you have access to both practical tools and inner wisdom. This trust becomes an anchor, allowing you to move forward with greater ease and clarity, even when the path ahead isn't fully illuminated.

Your financial journey is uniquely yours. While you can learn from others' experiences and wisdom, your path will unfold in its own way, guided by your particular combination of practical knowledge and intuitive knowledge. Trust in this unfolding. Trust that each step, whether it looks like progress or a detour, is contributing to your growth in financial wisdom.

As you continue to walk this path, you'll find that trusting the journey becomes less about forcing yourself to believe and more about recognizing the wisdom that's already guiding you. Your relationship with money transforms from one of struggle and control to one of partnership and flow, anchored in the deep understanding that you have everything you need to navigate your unique path to prosperity.

From Noise To Knowing

In our modern world, financial noise is constant and overwhelming. Market updates ping our phones, social media floods us with credit advice, and everyone seems to have an opinion about what we should do with our money. Moving from this cacophony of voices to clear inner knowing requires both intention and practice. It's about learning to tune your internal radio to the frequency of wisdom rather than static.

Clearing financial static begins with recognizing the various forms of noise that cloud your clarity. External static comes from obvious sources: financial media, well-meaning friends, social media feeds, and marketing messages. But there's also internal static: the mental chatter of worry, the emotional noise of past money trauma, and the persistent hum of societal beliefs about wealth and worth.

Start with a "Noise Audit" of your financial life. For one week, notice all the sources of money input you receive. Which voices demand your attention? Which opinions carry the most weight? What messages play on repeat in your mind? Don't try to eliminate these voices yet; simply become aware of them. Like tuning a radio, you must first identify the interference before you can find the clear channel.

Creating periods of financial silence becomes essential. This might mean implementing "money quiet hours," where you turn off financial notifications, unfollow financial influencers, or take social media breaks. Perhaps you designate certain days as "no money talk" days, focusing instead on simply observing your relationship with wealth and abundance. In these quiet spaces, your inner wisdom often begins to speak more clearly.

Accessing clear guidance requires developing discernment about which voices serve your highest good. Think of your intuition as a wise friend who whispers rather than shouts. While external advice often comes with urgency and pressure, inner wisdom tends to arrive with quiet certainty. It doesn't need to convince or persuade—it simply knows.

Practice listening for this wisdom in low-stakes situations first. Before checking your investment accounts, pause and notice what you already know about their status. Before opening a bill, tune into your sense of its contents. These small moments of practicing intuitive awareness build your capacity to access clear guidance when facing bigger decisions.

Pay attention to the quality of different forms of financial guidance. External advice often carries an energy of pushing or pulling—pushing you toward certain choices or pulling you away from others. Inner wisdom, by contrast, tends to have a centering quality. It draws you neither forward nor back but deeper into your own knowledge.

Making aligned choices becomes easier as you learn to distinguish between noise and knowledge. An aligned choice has a distinctive feel, a sense of rightness that goes beyond logic or emotion. It's as if all parts of you—body, mind, heart, and spirit—are nodding in agreement. This doesn't mean the choice is easy or without risk, but rather that it resonates with your deepest truth.

Start noticing the physical signatures of aligned decisions. Perhaps you experience a subtle expansion in your chest, a settling in your stomach, or a sense of energy flowing freely. These bodily responses are often more reliable than mental analysis alone, offering immediate feedback about alignment.

Create what I call "Alignment Anchors," personal practices that help you quickly return to your center when financial noise threatens to overwhelm your clarity. This might be a specific breath pattern, a grounding visualization, or a simple physical gesture that reminds you to check in with your inner wisdom before making decisions.

The ability to trust your path emerges naturally as you build a track record of listening to and acting upon your authentic wisdom. This trust isn't blind faith but rather a well-earned confidence in your ability to discern wisdom from noise. It's understanding that while the path may not always be clear, you have an inner compass that consistently points toward true north.

Remember that your financial path is unique. What looks like noise for you might be valuable guidance for someone else, and vice versa. The key is developing your personal filters—learning to recognize the specific frequency of your inner wisdom amid the general static of financial advice and opinion.

View this journey from noise to knowing as a spiral rather than a straight line. You'll likely revisit similar situations and decisions multiple times, each pass offering an opportunity to fine-tune your ability to access clear guidance. Sometimes, you'll slip back into old patterns of being overwhelmed by noise; this is part of the path, offering chances to practice returning to center.

You'll likely find that the journey transforms as you continue this practice. What began as an effort to make better financial decisions becomes a deeper exploration of trust, authenticity, and alignment. The noise begins to fade, not because it disappears but because your connection to your inner knowing grows stronger, clearer, and more reliable.

Eventually, you may discover that the most profound financial wisdom doesn't shout for attention or arrive with fanfare. It whispers in quiet moments, speaks through aligned opportunities, and guides you with a steady hand toward choices that serve not just your bank account but your whole being. This is the journey from noise to knowing—a path that leads not just to wiser money choices but to a more authentic and aligned relationship with wealth itself.

Wealth Wisdom Reflection:

1. When did your financial intuition prove right?

2. What's your money wisdom telling you now?

3. Where are you overriding your knowing?

4. What decision needs your deeper listening?

The $624,000 Awakening

In January 2018, my financial coach, Dr. Franchelle Ceasar, stared at a number that seemed to defy reality: $624,000 in debt. As a successful physician and mother, she'd done everything "right." She had earned her doctorate, built her career, and created a beautiful life for her young family. But that mountain of debt loomed over everything, threatening the future she envisioned for her toddlers.

Like many people facing financial crisis, Dr. Fran turned to conventional wisdom. Dave Ramsey's debt repayment strategy was supposed to be foolproof—a clear, step-by-step path to financial freedom. She threw herself into it with determined intensity, following every rule and guideline precisely.

By March, she found herself crying into her pillow each night, her spirit crushed under the weight of someone else's financial formula. The numbers might have been adding up, but something deeper wasn't working. One evening, watching her toddlers play, a realization hit her: Did she want their earliest memories to be of a mother consumed by misery, grinding through five years of joyless debt repayment?

That's when Dr. Fran did something radical. She got quiet and listened to her own financial wisdom. Instead of forcing herself into someone else's system, she honored her intuition about what would work for her family. Her plan wasn't conventional, but it aligned perfectly with her values, energy, and inner knowledge.

The results defied everyone's expectations. By March 2019—just twelve months after starting her self-designed journey—Dr. Fran had eliminated all $624,000 of debt, not by following an expert's blueprint but by trusting the wisdom that had been within her all along.

Today, Dr. Fran helps others find their path to financial freedom, teaching them that the most powerful financial strategies often come not from external experts but from the quiet voice of their own knowing.

Your deepest financial wisdom isn't something you need to learn—it's something you need to hear. As you develop this relationship with your inner knowing, you'll find yourself making decisions with more confidence and less struggle. In the next chapter, we'll explore how to turn this wisdom into a bold vision for your future, but first, take a moment to listen. What is your money wisdom trying to tell you right now?

KEY TAKEAWAYS:
- Financial intuition is as valuable as logical analysis
- Inner wisdom combines experience and insight
- Different levels of financial guidance exist
- Quiet listening reveals deeper financial truth

CHAPTER 5

Speaking Your Money Truth

"You really don't need to pay me," I said, waving away yet another request for an invoice. "Just pay it forward. Put everything you learned from me into practice, then teach it to someone else." The words flowed easily, wrapped in the noble cloak of generosity. After all, I reasoned, I had a comfortable salary as a soldier. Why should I charge for helping others transform their financial lives?

My client shifted uncomfortably in her chair. "But I want to pay you. You have literally changed everything for me. I finally understand how to break free from this debt that has been strangling me."

I smiled, feeling that familiar warm glow of making a difference while simultaneously dismissing my own worth. "Really, knowing I helped you is my payment."

This scene played out dozens of times in my early days as a financial coach. In our sessions, people would experience profound transformations—breaking through money blocks, developing their first realistic budget, creating debt freedom plans, and improving their credit. When they reached for their wallet, I'd stop them with what I thought was selfless generosity.

I didn't recognize it then, but refusing to accept payment wasn't just about generosity. It was my money voice speaking volumes through its silence. Every declined invoice, every deflected attempt at compensation, every "pay it forward" was really saying: "My expertise isn't worth monetary recognition. My time isn't valuable enough to charge for. My impact isn't significant enough to warrant payment."

The irony wasn't lost on me. Here I was, teaching others about financial empowerment while demonstrating the opposite through my actions. I was showing them how to value money while devaluing my contribution to their success.

The turning point came during a conversation with my mentor. When I proudly shared how many people I was helping for free, expecting praise for my generosity, she instead asked a question that stopped me in my tracks: "How does refusing payment honor your clients' desire to express gratitude? How does it model healthy financial relationships?"

Her words cracked open something in me. I realized that by refusing payment, I wasn't just diminishing my worth; I was denying my clients the dignity of fair exchange. I was inadvertently teaching them that valuable financial guidance shouldn't cost anything and that expertise in money matters wasn't worth paying for.

Today, I state my rates clearly, send invoices promptly, and accept payment gratefully—not because I need the money more than I did then, but because I understand that clear financial voices speak in both directions. When I honor my worth, I give others permission to honor theirs. When I accept fair compensation, I demonstrate what healthy financial relationships look like.

That transformation—from declining payment to confidently stating my rates—wasn't just about money. It was about finding my financial voice and aligning my actions with the principles I was teaching. It was about recognizing that true generosity includes being generous with ourselves and that real financial empowerment begins with clearly expressing our worth.

Your money has a voice—not just in what you say about it but in how you say it.

It speaks in the tremor when you name your price.

It echoes in the silence when you should be asking for more.

It whispers in the apologies that precede your rates.

But what if you could speak your money truth with the same confidence you feel about your expertise?

What if your voice carried the full weight of your worth?

Finding Your Financial Voice

Money speaks through us long before we consciously choose its words. From our earliest experiences, we absorbed the financial language of our environment—the hushed conversations about bills, the proud declarations of savings, or perhaps the tense silences around spending. This inherited money language shapes how we express our own financial reality today, but it may not truly reflect who we are or who we want to become.

The difference between learned money language and authentic expression lies in awareness. When we speak from learned patterns, we might echo our parents' anxieties about money or repeat cultural myths about wealth that don't align with our values. Authentic financial expression, however, emerges from our current reality—our actual relationship with money, our genuine worth, and our present financial goals.

Your money voice directly impacts your wealth in ways that extend far beyond simple transactions. When you speak with uncertainty about your rates, that hesitation often translates into lower earnings. When you clearly articulate your value, it opens doors to opportunities that match your worth. The energy and confidence in your financial voice become self-fulfilling prophecies, either reinforcing limitations or expanding possibilities.

Breaking free from inherited money scripts requires conscious examination of your current financial language. Notice when you automatically apologize for your prices or shrink from discussions about money. These patterns often trace back to early messages about what was "appropriate" or "polite" regarding money talk. Recognition is the first step towards change.

Your authentic financial tone emerges gradually, like an instrument finding its natural resonance. It might feel uncomfortable at first—speaking clearly about money often does when we're used to softening our words—but this voice carries your truth: your professional expertise, value in the marketplace, and right to fair compensation.

This authenticity doesn't mean being rigid or harsh. Your financial voice can be firm and compassionate, clear and considerate. It's about finding the tone that aligns with your values. Sometimes, it whispers, sometimes it projects, but it always speaks your truth.

Think of your financial voice as a muscle that strengthens with use. Each time you state your rates without apology, hold a boundary around payment terms, and negotiate from a place of confidence, you're developing this crucial aspect of your financial well-being.

Consider how your financial voice might sound when it's fully aligned with your worth. What would change in your business conversations or salary negotiations? How would you discuss money with loved ones? What agreements would you make—or break? This voice, your authentic financial voice, is ready to emerge. It simply needs your permission to speak.

The Language of Confidence

Understanding your money voice pattern is the first step towards transformation. The impact of finding your financial voice is measurable. A 2023 Glassdoor survey reveals that 63% of workers who successfully negotiated their salary increased their compensation by more than 10%. Moreover, a 2023 Fidelity study shows that 65% of couples who communicate regularly about finances report higher relationship satisfaction. Your money voice doesn't just affect your income; it influences every financial relationship in your life.

These common archetypes represent different ways we've learned to communicate about our worth, each with its own characteristic phrases, behaviors, and underlying beliefs.

The Apologetic Achiever

Despite significant accomplishments and expertise, the Apologetic Achiever leads with uncertainty. You might recognize this pattern if you frequently begin money conversations with "I'm sorry, but..." or "I hate to ask, but..." This voice pattern often belongs to highly skilled professionals who have yet to fully own their worth.

Listen closely, and you'll hear their expertise wrapped in doubt: "I know this might seem high, but..." or "I'm still learning, but my rate is..." The Apologetic Achiever's language diminishes their value before others have a chance to respond. Their emails overflow with exclamation points and qualifiers, attempting to soften the impact of their financial requests.

The Silent Sufferer

This pattern manifests as avoidance and accommodation. The Silent Sufferer will accept unfair payment terms, delay invoicing, or take on extra work without compensation—all while saying nothing. Their silence comes at a cost, building resentment that eventually affects their work and relationships.

The Silent Sufferer's voice emerges subtly: the unasked questions in meetings, the unbilled hours on projects, and the unsigned contracts that should be reviewed. When they do speak, it's often too late, after boundaries have been crossed and patterns have been established.

The Defensive Discounter

Quick to justify and quicker to discount, this pattern reveals a deep-seated belief that value must be proven rather than stated. The Defensive Discounter rushes to explain their rates before anyone questions them, often offering reductions before they're requested.

Their language is heavy with justification: "I know I should charge more, but..." or "I can offer a discount if..." They might list their credentials unprompted or provide detailed breakdowns of their time—all signs of seeking external validation for their worth.

The Confident Claimer

This is the voice pattern we're all working toward. The Confident Claimer states their rates clearly, sets boundaries respectfully, and easily navigates money conversations. Their language is direct without being harsh and firm without being rigid.

Listen for their clear, uncomplicated statements: "My rate for this project is..." or "Here's how I structure my payments..." They ask questions when needed and maintain comfortable silence while waiting for responses. Their confidence comes not from arrogance but from a deep understanding of their value.

Where Do You Recognize Yourself?

Most of us can find elements of multiple patterns in our money voice, often shifting between them depending on the situation. You might be a Confident Claimer in low-stakes situations but slip into Apologetic Achiever mode when the numbers get bigger. Perhaps you're generally confident but become a Silent Sufferer with specific clients or family members.

Take a moment to reflect on your most recent money conversations. Which patterns feel familiar? When do you notice yourself shifting between them? Understanding your current patterns isn't about judgment; it's about awareness. Each pattern served a purpose in your journey, helping you navigate financial conversations in the best way you knew how at the time.

Remember that these patterns are learned behaviors, not fixed traits. The Apologetic Achiever can learn to state their worth clearly. The Silent Sufferer can find their voice. The Defensive Discounter can trust in their value. Every Confident Claimer started somewhere else; they simply consciously chose to change their money voice.

Your pattern is your starting point, not your destination. With awareness and practice, you can develop a new money voice that truly reflects your worth and supports your financial growth.

Transformational Moment: The Money Voice Declaration

Find a quiet space where you won't be interrupted. Whether you're a business owner, corporate professional, or transitioning between roles, this exercise will help you develop a more confident financial voice. Have a journal ready— this is a moment you'll want to document.

Step 1: The Mirror Moment

Stand in front of a mirror. Take three deep breaths, grounding yourself in your expertise, experience, and value. Look directly into your own eyes. This might feel uncomfortable—stay with that feeling. It's where growth begins.

Without looking away, state your value proposition. Choose the one most relevant to your situation:

For Corporate Professionals: "My annual compensation should be [amount]." "My skills and experience merit a [percentage] raise." "My contribution to this team is worth [amount]."

For Business Owners: "My rate is [amount]." "My monthly retainer is [amount]." "My minimum project fee is [amount]."

Step 2: The Boundary Statement

Now, still maintaining eye contact with yourself, state one clear professional boundary. Choose one that you often struggle to maintain.

For Corporate Professionals: "I require compensation for overtime hours." "My scope of responsibilities needs to reflect my position." "I expect my bonus to reflect my performance metrics."

For Business Owners: "Payment is required before work begins." "I don't offer discounts on this service." "Rush fees apply to projects with less than [time frame] notice."

Step 3: The Worth Declaration

Place one hand over your heart. Complete these statements, speaking them with conviction:

Universal Declarations:
"I create value by..."
"My expertise is worth..."
"My time and energy deserve..."
"I no longer need to justify..."
"I choose to believe..."

Step 4: The Financial Need Expression

Practice these statements, adjusting them to fit your situation:

For Corporate Professionals:
"To advance my career, I need..."
"To reflect my contribution, my salary should be..."
"To maintain work-life balance, my compensation must..."

For Business Owners:
"To grow my business, I need..."
"To serve my clients best, my fee must be..."
"To honor my worth, I require..."

Step 5: The Power Phrases

Create three power phrases that feel authentic to you. Write them in your journal.

For Corporate Professionals: For salary discussions: "Based on my performance and market research, I'm seeking..."

For role expansion: "Given my additional responsibilities, let's discuss compensation..."

For negotiations: "My qualifications and experience align with a salary of..."

For Business Owners: For pricing: "My rate reflects the value and results I deliver."

For boundaries: "Let me explain how I structure my payment terms."

For negotiations: "That's outside my standard pricing structure."

Step 6: The Integration

Take a seat and write in your journal:

Which statements felt most challenging?

Where did you feel physical resistance?

Which declarations gave you a sense of power?

What surprised you about this exercise?

Step 7: The Daily Practice

Choose one declaration that feels both challenging and exciting. Write it on a card or set a private reminder on your phone. For the next 21 days, speak this declaration aloud each morning. Track how your delivery changes, your confidence grows, and your belief in these words deepens.

Final Integration

Close this exercise by standing once more before the mirror. State your full worth declaration:

For Corporate Professionals: "I am [name], and my professional value merits [amount/level]. I maintain clear boundaries because I respect my worth and my organization's success. My compensation reflects my expertise, and I discuss it with confidence. I choose to speak my career truth clearly, professionally, and without apology."

For Business Owners: "I am [name], and my work is valued at [amount]. I maintain clear financial boundaries because I respect my worth and clients' success. My rates reflect my expertise, and I state them with confidence. I choose to speak my money truth clearly, confidently, and without apology."

Remember: This declaration isn't just words—it's a new way of being with money and worth.

Return to this exercise whenever you need to reinforce your professional voice, whether preparing for a performance review, salary negotiation, or client meeting. Each time you practice, your confidence grows stronger, your voice becomes clearer, and your worth becomes more firmly anchored in your being.

Your professional voice is ready to speak its truth. All you need to do is give it permission to be heard.

Sacred Boundaries

Financial boundaries aren't just business decisions; they're acts of profound self-respect. Like the walls of a temple, they protect something sacred: your worth, energy, and financial well-being. Yet, for many, setting and maintaining these boundaries feels like an act of defiance rather than the act of self-love it truly is.

Why Financial Boundaries Are Acts of Self-Love

You make a powerful declaration of self-worth each time you honor your financial boundaries. Think of boundaries as loving agreements you make with yourself first, then share with others. When you say "no" to working below your rate, you say "yes" to your value. When you enforce payment terms, you honor your need for security and respect.

These boundaries do more than protect your bank account—they preserve your energy, safeguard your time, and maintain the quality of your work. They ensure you have the resources necessary to serve at your highest level, whether serving your clients, your employer, or your own growth.

Consider what happens without these loving limits: resentment builds, quality suffers, and financial well-being becomes compromised. By setting clear boundaries, you're not just protecting yourself; you're creating the conditions necessary for genuine prosperity and sustainable success.

Creating Boundaries That Honor Your Worth

Start by identifying your non-negotiables. These are the fundamental standards that protect your financial well-being:

- The minimum rate that honors your expertise

- The payment terms that support your cash flow

- The scope limits that protect your energy

- The response times that respect your balance

- The financial agreements that ensure clarity

Write these boundaries down as loving commitments to yourself; frame them positively. Instead of "I won't work for less," try "I choose projects that value my expertise at [amount]." Rather than "I don't do rush jobs," consider "I maintain quality by allowing [timeframe] for projects."

Communicating Limits with Grace

The art of boundary-setting lies not just in what you say but also in how you say it. Firm doesn't mean harsh. Clear doesn't mean inflexible. Your boundaries can be both strong and gracious, much like a host who clearly states when dinner will end.

Practice phrases that combine clarity with kindness:

"I understand your budget constraints. Let me share what I can offer within that range..."

"To ensure I deliver my best work, my payment structure is..."

"I value our relationship, which is why I want to be clear about..."

Remember that you're not just stating rules; you're sharing your professional standards. When explained from this perspective, boundaries become invitations to a better working relationship rather than limitations.

Standing Firm in Your Financial Truth

The true test of boundaries comes when they're challenged. This is where many of us falter, where the old voices of doubt creep in. Remember, standing firm isn't about being rigid—it's about being reliable, first to yourself and then to others.

Recall your "why" when pressure arises to lower your rates, extend payment terms, or blur scope boundaries. Ground yourself in the self-love that inspired these boundaries. Your response can be both compassionate and clear:

"I understand this isn't the fit you were hoping for. I'm happy to refer you to someone who might better match your budget."

"My rates reflect the value I provide and the expertise I bring. I'm confident in the results we'll achieve at this investment level."

Your boundaries will be tested. See these moments not as confrontations but as opportunities to practice self-love in action. Each time you maintain a boundary with grace, you strengthen your financial foundation and demonstrate what healthy professional relationships look like.

Remember, your financial boundaries are sacred agreements. They're not walls to keep others out but clear markers that show them how to engage with you professionally. By honoring them, you teach others how to honor them, too.

When doubt arises, return to this truth: Your boundaries are acts of love—love for your work, those you serve, and most importantly, love for yourself. In maintaining them, you create the space for true prosperity to flourish.

Your financial boundaries are not just about money. They're about dignity, respect, and recognizing your inherent worth. Stand firm in this truth, communicate it gracefully, and watch how your professional relationships transform.

Empowered Decisions

The journey from seeking permission to claiming power is perhaps the most profound transformation in our financial lives. It's the moment when we stop looking outside ourselves for validation of our money choices and begin trusting our inner financial wisdom.

Moving from Permission to Power

Think back to your last significant financial decision. Did you seek multiple opinions before acting? Did you need someone else to validate your choice? While counsel has its place, the habit of seeking permission often masks a deeper hesitation to trust ourselves.

Permission-seeking weaves through our financial lives in subtle ways. We run our rates past others before quoting them, as if someone else holds the key to our worth. We question whether we "deserve" a raise before requesting one, waiting for external validation of our value. We search for the "right time" to invest in ourselves, looking for guarantees before making money moves.

True financial empowerment begins when you recognize that you are the ultimate authority on your money choices. Others can advise, but you must decide. This shift from external validation to internal trust transforms your decisions and your entire relationship with money.

Making Unapologetic Money Choices

Unapologetic doesn't mean reckless or inconsiderate. It means owning your choices fully, without the need to justify or explain them excessively. Consider the energy difference between these approaches:

When raising rates, replace "I'm thinking about raising my rates, if that's okay..." with "My new rates will take effect next quarter."

When investing in growth, transform "I might need to invest in this training program..." into "I'm investing in my growth through this program."

Your voice carries power when it comes from a place of ownership rather than doubt. Practice making clear money statements that reflect your authority: "This is what I'm choosing to do with my money." Feel how different this feels from apologetic or permission-seeking language. Let your words emerge from a place of clarity rather than defense.

Trusting Your Financial Judgment

Your financial judgment has been building through every experience – positive and negative – in your money story. Even the choices that didn't work out as planned have contributed to your wisdom. Those moments when an investment didn't yield expected returns or a client relationship didn't align with your worth weren't failures. They were deposits in your wisdom account, each one strengthening your ability to make more aligned choices.

Begin recognizing the expertise you've developed through lived experience. What patterns have emerged in your financial life? Which decisions have served you well? Your intuition speaks through these patterns, whispering guidance based on years of real-world experience. Create space each day to listen to this inner knowledge. Let it remind you that you've been building trustworthy financial judgment all along.

Consider starting a Financial Wisdom Journal, not as a ledger of transactions but as a living record of your insights and successful decisions. Return to these pages when doubt creeps in. Let them remind you that you've been building trustworthy financial judgment all along.

Leading with Confidence

Financial leadership begins with leading yourself. This means making decisions based on your values, not others' expectations. It means taking action from a place of clarity rather than fear. When you stand firm in your choices while remaining open to learning, you set the tone for how others engage with you about money.

Your financial leadership voice might say, "I've considered this carefully and decided..." or "This aligns with my financial strategy." Notice how these statements carry both authority and openness. They acknowledge that while you've done your due diligence, you're not seeking approval or permission.

This confident stance ripples out, affecting your money choices and how others perceive and respond to you financially. Leadership doesn't mean never having doubts—it means moving forward thoughtfully despite them. Your confidence grows with each decisive action, each boundary honored, and each value-aligned choice.

When resistance appears—and it will—remember that discomfort is normal when claiming new power. Others' reactions often reflect their own money stories, not your worthiness to make bold choices. You don't need everyone to understand your decisions. You need only to understand them yourself.

Each morning, affirm one financial truth that grounds you in your power. Make one money decision without seeking validation. Celebrate one moment of financial leadership. Document one instance of trusting your judgment. These aren't just activities—they're investments in your financial sovereignty.

Remember, empowered decisions aren't about being right all the time. They're about taking full ownership of your financial journey. You strengthen this sovereignty whenever you make a clear money choice, honor your judgment, or lead confidently. Your money decisions are yours to make. You've earned this power through every financial lesson, every mistake, and every success. Now it's time to claim it fully, lead with it confidently, and watch how it transforms not just your finances but your entire relationship with your worth.

The path to financial empowerment asks you to trust yourself first, let your inner wisdom guide your choices, and stand firmly in your truth—even when others question your path. As you practice this trust, you'll find your financial voice growing stronger, your choices becoming clearer, and your relationship with money transforming into one of partnership rather than permission-seeking.

Building Your Money Confidence

Every financial transformation begins with small, deliberate steps. Building your money confidence is like developing any other skill, requiring awareness, practice, and consistent reinforcement. Let's walk through each crucial stage of this journey.

1. Recognizing Your Current Voice

Take a week to observe your financial language without judgment. How do you respond when someone asks about your rates? What words tumble out when discussing money with family? Notice the subtle patterns: the automatic "sorry" before stating your price, the urge to justify your fees with a lengthy explanation, or perhaps the tendency to stay silent when you should speak up.

Keep a "voice journal" for seven days. Write down your exact words in money conversations. Include the physical sensations that arise: the tightness in your throat, the racing heart, the downward gaze. This awareness creates a baseline for growth and helps identify which specific patterns need attention.

2. Practicing New Money Language

Now, it's time to consciously reshape your money vocabulary. Create your personal "power phrases"—clear, confident statements that reflect your worth. Instead of "I hope this price is okay," try "My rate for this service is..." Rather than "I know it's expensive, but..." simply state, "The investment for this project is..."

Start with written communication. Draft email templates that embody your desired money voice. Practice saying your rates out loud until they feel as natural as introducing yourself. Record yourself stating prices and play it back. Listen not just to the words but to the tone. Does it convey certainty or authority? Keep practicing until it does.

3. Setting Clear Boundaries

Your financial boundaries communicate your professional value. Implement non-negotiable standards: minimum project rates, payment schedules, and scope limitations. Write these down as policies, not suggestions. For example: "Payment is due upon project completion" becomes "Full payment is required within 7 days of invoice date."

Test these boundaries in low-risk situations first. When a client asks for "just one small addition" to a project, respond with your scope change policy. When someone requests a discount, refer to your clear pricing structure. Each time you maintain a boundary, you strengthen your money confidence.

4. Making Confident Requests

Start making requests that stretch your comfort zone. Begin with simple asks: "I'd like to review the terms of my credit card." Progress to bolder statements: "Based on my performance, I'm requesting a 15% salary increase." Frame each request as a professional proposition rather than a personal favor.

Prepare for these conversations in advance. Write down your key points. Practice with a trusted friend or mentor. Remember that every "no" builds resilience, and every "yes" confirms your worth. The goal isn't perfection; it's progress in advocating for your financial needs.

5. Celebrating Your Growth

Create a "Money Voice Victory Log." Document every instance where you spoke up about money with confidence. Did you quote your full rate without flinching? Write it down. Did you maintain a boundary when pressured to discount? That's a victory. Did you negotiate better terms on a contract? Celebrate it.

Set regular check-ins with yourself to review your progress. Compare your current money conversations with those you documented in week one. Notice the evolution in your language, tone, and confidence. Share your wins with a supportive community that understands the significance of these shifts.

Remember, building money confidence isn't linear. Some days, you'll speak with unwavering certainty; others, you might struggle to find your voice. This is normal. What matters is your commitment to growth and your willingness to keep practicing, even when it feels uncomfortable.

Each time you speak confidently about money, you're not just building your financial voice; you're creating a new model for others. Your growth ripples out, showing colleagues, clients, and even family members what healthy money conversations can look like. This isn't just about personal transformation; it's about contributing to a larger cultural shift in discussing and relating to money.

The Power of Clear Communication

Clear communication about money isn't just about the words we choose—it's about creating an understanding that builds trust, respect, and mutually beneficial relationships. When we learn to speak about money with clarity, we transform our financial outcomes and the very nature of our professional and personal connections.

Having Difficult Money Conversations

The conversations we fear most are often the ones we most need to have. Whether discussing a past-due invoice, requesting a raise, or addressing financial expectations with family, these moments shape our financial future. The key lies not in avoiding discomfort but in moving through it with purpose and grace.

Begin these conversations by stating your intention: "I want to discuss something important to ensure we're aligned." Then, present the facts without emotion: "According to our agreement, payment was due last week." Follow with a clear, solution-focused request: "I'd like to establish a plan to bring this current and prevent future delays."

Notice how this approach differs from either apologetic hedging or aggressive demands. It creates space for dialogue while maintaining professional standards.

Negotiating with Confidence

Negotiation becomes natural when we view it as a collaborative exploration rather than a battle. Start by understanding your non-negotiables—those elements that truly matter to your financial well-being. Express these clearly: "My rate reflects both my expertise and the value I deliver to your organization."

When counteroffers come, respond from a place of certainty rather than scarcity: "I appreciate your position. Here's what I can offer within those constraints." This maintains both the relationship and worthwhile exploration of possibilities.

Remember that silence can be your strongest tool in negotiations. After stating your position, resist the urge to fill the space with justifications. Let your worth speak for itself.

Setting Prices Without Fear

Price-setting becomes clearer when we understand it's not just about numbers— it's about the value exchange we create. Consider what transformation you offer. What problems do you solve? What relief do you provide? Let these guide your pricing discussions.

When sharing prices, use simple, direct language: "The investment for this project is..." Notice how different this feels from "I charge..." or "My price is..." Small language shifts can significantly impact how others perceive and receive your rates.

The fear in pricing often comes from anticipating objections. Instead of defending before you're questioned, lead with value: "This investment includes... and delivers..." This frames the conversation around *worth* rather than *cost*.

Discussing Wealth Without Shame

Our culture carries complex messages about wealth that often make us hesitant to discuss money openly and honestly. Yet clear communication about wealth builds understanding and opportunities for growth.

When discussing financial success, speak from a place of gratitude and responsibility rather than ego or apology. "I've been fortunate to build this level of security, and I'm committed to using it wisely." This acknowledges abundance while remaining grounded and relatable.

Share your financial journey with authenticity, including victories and learning moments. This will create connection and permit others to engage honestly about their relationship with wealth.

The Power of Financial Storytelling

Every financial discussion tells a story—about value, relationships, and possibilities. Learn to craft these stories intentionally. Instead of "I can't afford that," try "I'm choosing to invest my resources elsewhere." Rather than "That's too expensive," consider "I'd rather not make that a financial priority at this time."

These narratives shape how others understand our choices and how we understand them ourselves. Clear communication becomes a tool for both external negotiation and internal alignment.

Integration and Practice

The path to clearer financial communication begins with awareness. Notice your default patterns in money conversations. Where do you tend to hedge or apologize? Where might directness serve better than explanation?

First, practice new approaches in low-stakes situations. Perhaps start by stating your coffee order without the usual "just" or "only." Notice how it feels to make clear requests without diminishing them.

Remember that clear communication serves everyone. When you speak clearly about money, you create a model for others to follow. This ripple effect transforms individual conversations and our collective relationship with financial dialogue.

Your voice carries power—the power to transform understanding, create clarity, and build authentic financial relationships. Use it wisely and clearly, and watch how the quality of your money conversations transforms.

Wealth Wisdom Reflection:

1. How does your money voice change in different situations?
2. What financial boundaries need strengthening?
3. Where are you still seeking permission?
4. What truth are you ready to speak?

Finding Her Voice, Claiming Her Worth

"A raise? Doesn't your husband make a lot of money? Why do you want a raise?"

The words hung in the air of the small office, sharp and dismissive. Natalie felt heat rise to her cheeks, her hands trembling slightly as she stood before her employer. Four years. Four years of dedicated service without a single raise. Four years of running the company with precision, of being the backbone that kept everything flowing smoothly. Four years of silence.

But today was different. Today, Natalie had walked into this office carrying something new: the certainty of her worth. She had prepared meticulously for this conversation, rehearsing her talking points, gathering evidence of her contributions, and steeling herself for negotiation. What she hadn't prepared for was having her professional worth reduced to her marital status.

The familiar urge to shrink, apologize, and retreat washed over her. For a moment, she felt the weight of every woman who had ever been dismissed, every professional whose value had been tied to something other than their merit. But something else rose stronger within her—a voice that had been growing steadily, nurtured by the recognition of her power.

Her employer stood there, seemingly confident in the righteousness of her questioning. The silence stretched between them, a space where old patterns of acquiescence might have once rushed in. But Natalie filled that space with something else: her truth.

"My husband's income has nothing to do with my expertise or the time I put into this company," Natalie responded, her voice steady and clear. "It is only fair that I am properly compensated for my contributions to this company."

No defense. No justification. No apology. Just a clean, clear statement of worth.

In that moment, something shifted—not just in the dynamic between employer and employee but also in Natalie's own relationship with her value. By claiming her worth out loud and refusing to let personal circumstances diminish her professional value, she had done more than secure a raise. She had found her money voice.

The raise she requested was approved. But the real victory wasn't in the numbers on her paycheck—it was in how she stood her ground, separated her professional worth from her personal circumstances, and spoke her truth without flinching.

Natalie's story reminds us that our money voice often finds its strength in moments of challenge. It grows not from the absence of fear but from choosing to speak through it. Her journey from silence to strength, from acceptance to advocacy, mirrors the path many of us must take to claim our financial voice.

Sometimes, all it takes is one moment of standing firm in your truth to transform your financial reality and your entire relationship with your worth. Natalie's voice that day did more than secure fair compensation. It declared that her value was inherent, professional, and entirely her own.

From Silence To Strength

The journey from financial silence to strength isn't always linear. It's a spiral path of growing awareness, occasional setbacks, and the continued emergence of your authentic money voice. Each time you speak your truth, you heal not just your own relationship with money but create ripples of possibility for others.

Overcoming Money Shame

Money shame whispers that we should stay quiet about our financial struggles or success. It tells us that wanting more is greedy, that asking for our worth is unseemly, and that discussing money is somehow wrong. This shame keeps us trapped in patterns of silence that serve no one.

Freedom begins when we recognize these whispers as inherited stories, not truths. Your desire for financial well-being isn't greed—it's a healthy expression of self-worth. Your need to discuss money isn't inappropriate—it's necessary for creating clear agreements and sustainable relationships.

Start by naming your money shame aloud: "I felt ashamed when I couldn't pay that bill." "I feel uncomfortable when others know my success." Speaking these truths, even to yourself in the mirror, begins to dissolve their power. Each acknowledgment creates space for a new story where your financial voice deserves to be heard.

Building Voice Resilience

Your money voice, like any muscle, grows stronger through conscious use. The first time you state your rates without apologizing might feel terrifying. The twentieth time still might flutter your heart. By the hundredth time, you'll wonder why it ever seemed so hard.

Resilience doesn't mean never feeling fear; it means speaking through it. When your voice shakes while requesting payment, speak anyway. When doubt creeps in during a negotiation, stay present anyway. When old patterns of silence tempt you, choose expression anyway.

Create a resilience practice. Start by speaking one financial truth aloud each day. Perhaps it's your ideal income, a boundary you're setting, or a money goal you're claiming. Let your voice carry these intentions into the world, even if, at first, only your own ears hear them.

Creating Lasting Change

Sustainable transformation emerges from aligned action, not just good intentions. Your money voice grows stronger when your actions match your words, your boundaries align with your values, and your choices reflect your worth.

Notice the small daily moments where you can choose strength over silence. When someone asks your rate, state it clearly instead of hedging. When a boundary feels uncomfortable, maintain it anyway. When an opportunity doesn't match your worth, decline it gracefully.

Document your journey. Write down each victory, no matter how small.
"Today, I said no to an undervalued opportunity."
"Today, I stated my rate without apologizing."
"Today, I had a difficult money conversation with grace."
These moments compound, creating a foundation for lasting change.

Leading by Example

As your money voice strengthens, you become a living permission slip for others to find their voice. Your clear boundaries show colleagues what healthy professional relationships look like. Your confident rate discussions demonstrate how to honor both yourself and your clients. Your honest conversations about money create space for others to speak their truth.

Leadership doesn't require perfection. Share your journey, including the struggles. Let others see that finding your money voice is a process, that strength emerges from practice, and that change is possible at any point in your financial story.

Extend the same compassion you needed on your journey when you encounter someone still trapped in silence. Share your story if asked. Offer encouragement when appropriate. Remember that your example speaks louder than any advice.

Your journey from silence to strength ripples out far beyond your own life. Each time you speak with financial clarity, you help create a world where money conversations can be honest, worth can be claimed, and voices can be heard.

The path forward isn't about becoming someone new. It's about allowing your authentic voice to emerge and trusting that your financial truth deserves expression. It's about knowing that your voice can remain powerful and gracious even as it grows stronger.

Remember, your journey from silence to strength isn't just personal transformation; it's cultural change in action. Each time you speak your money truth, you help create a world where financial voices can be clear, worth can be claimed without shame, and strength can coexist with compassion.

Your voice matters. Your truth matters. Your journey from silence to strength matters. Keep speaking, keep growing, keep leading by example. The world needs your money voice in all its authentic, evolving, strengthening glory.

Your money voice isn't just about what you say—it's about who you become when you speak your truth. As you strengthen this voice, you'll make different choices, create stronger boundaries, and build deeper confidence. In the next chapter, we'll explore how to turn this voice into visionary action, but first, take a moment to listen to your own money voice. What truth is it ready to speak?

KEY TAKEAWAYS:
- Your money voice influences your financial outcomes
- Clear communication creates better financial results
- Confident money conversations build wealth
- Speaking truth transforms financial relationships

CHAPTER 6

Crafting Your Bold Vision

The air mattress wheezed beneath me as I shifted positions, trying to find comfort on my makeshift bed in Queens, NY. Such a far cry from my childhood dreams in Trinidad, where I'd lose myself in books that painted pictures of abundant possibilities. Now, here I was: hungry, broken, sharing a cramped two-bedroom apartment with seven others, my own space barely big enough for the air mattress that served as my bed, chair, and desk.

On this particular winter night in 2011, my tears fell silently in the darkness. The beautiful family I shared the apartment with couldn't know their strong, always-smiling housemate was crumbling. But then something shifted—a surge of defiant hope cut through my despair like a blade of light.

I jumped up, wiped my tears on my sleeping clothes, grabbed my pen and notepad, and began writing almost desperately. Not about my current reality but about the home I knew in my bones I would one day own. I could see it clearly: expansive windows framing breathtaking views, four bedrooms filled with warmth and life, a two-car garage symbolizing prosperity and choice. My pen raced across the paper, each detail a declaration of faith in my future.

With shaking hands, I opened my laptop. The screen's glow illuminated my tiny corner as I searched for homes matching my vision. Each photo I found and saved was an act of defiance against my circumstances. Here I was, without money for food, sleeping on a floor in a space meant for a baby's crib, yet daring to craft a vision that would make most people call me delusional.

But I knew something they didn't. Dreams aren't built on current circumstances but on the unwavering conviction that a greater reality is possible. My heart was bruised, but my vision remained unbreakable. At that moment, on that cold floor in Queens, I chose to believe in the impossible. And that choice would change everything.

There's a difference between a financial goal and a wealth vision. Goals live in spreadsheets. Visions live in your soul.

When was the last time your financial future made you catch your breath with excitement? When did you last feel your heart race thinking about what's possible? If your answer is "never" or "not lately," you're not alone. We've been taught to be "realistic" about money, to set "sensible" goals, and to dream "responsibly."

But here's the truth: The size of your vision determines the size of your results.

Most of us have been trained to approach our financial future with spreadsheets and calculators. We've learned to set goals based on our current income and maybe a modest percentage increase. We budget, forecast, and plan—all within the safe confines of what seems "reasonable." But this traditional approach fails us in profound ways.

Traditional financial planning starts with where you are and takes small steps forward. It asks questions like "What can I afford?" and "How much should I save each month?" While these questions have their place, they keep you trapped in your current reality. They anchor you to your present circumstances rather than pulling you toward a compelling future. The conventional approach starts with current limitations, focuses on scarcity and trade-offs, and creates incremental progress, at best. It keeps you playing in the realm of the predictable, generating minimal emotional engagement. This is why so many financial plans are abandoned in desk drawers or forgotten in computer files.

A soul-aligned vision operates on entirely different principles. Instead of starting with what's possible, it begins with what's desirable. Rather than asking, "What can I afford?" it asks, "What would light me up?" This shift changes everything. When your financial future is aligned with your soul's deepest desires, you tap into wellsprings of creativity, motivation, and resilience you didn't know you had. Money becomes not just about numbers but about meaning, not just about accumulation, but about impact. A vision that connects to your deeper purpose activates emotional engagement, unleashes creative problem-solving, and sustains long-term motivation. Perhaps most importantly, it attracts unexpected opportunities that a conventional plan would never have considered.

The greatest barrier to wealth creation isn't lack of opportunity—it's self-imposed limitations disguised as 'being realistic.' We've been conditioned to equate realism with wisdom, to see modest goals as mature and ambitious visions as naive. Yet Harvard Business Review's 2023 research validates the power of bold vision, showing that executives who document their goals and vision are 42% more likely to achieve them. Furthermore, a 2023 Prudential Financial Wellness study found that people with written financial goals are twice as likely to feel confident about their financial future. This isn't just about planning; it's about giving yourself permission to dream bigger than your current circumstances.

Here's what we forget: Every major innovation, every fortune created, every empire built started as an "unrealistic" vision. The world's greatest achievements began with someone daring to think beyond what seemed possible. Breaking free from realistic thinking requires questioning our inherited beliefs about money and challenging our assumptions about what's possible. It means separating probability from possibility and embracing the discomfort of bigger thinking. Most importantly, it means letting our desires lead our planning instead of letting our fears constrain them.

When you create from probability, you look at past patterns and project them forward. When you create from possibility, you start with your vision and work backward to make it real. Possibility thinking asks what could be rather than what has been. It invites you to imagine what you would create if you weren't afraid to fail, how your vision might become a reality, and what resources, skills, or connections might make this possible. It encourages you to study those who have already achieved something similar, not to copy their path but to expand your sense of what's possible.

This shift from probability to possibility thinking doesn't mean abandoning practical considerations. Instead, it means letting your vision drive your strategy rather than letting current circumstances limit your vision. Think of your bold vision as a powerful magnet, pulling you toward its realization. Your job isn't to figure out every step in advance. Your job is to create a vision so compelling that it inspires you to find a way, even when the path isn't clear.

The difference between traditional goal-setting and vision-based wealth creation is the difference between walking and flying. Both will get you somewhere, but they operate under completely different rules and create vastly different results. As you move through this chapter, give yourself permission to think bigger than you ever have before. Let your soul, not your spreadsheet, guide your financial future. Because when your vision is truly aligned with your deepest desires, you'll find yourself doing things you never thought possible to make it real.

The Anatomy Of A Bold Vision

Goals and visions share some DNA, but they're fundamentally different creatures. You can write a goal on a to-do list: save $50,000, buy a house, or start a business. Conversely, a vision is the story of a future that pulls you forward with magnetic force. It's the difference between "I want to start a business" and "I see myself building an empire that transforms an industry while creating opportunities for thousands." Goals exist in the realm of doing. Visions exist in the realm of becoming.

The most compelling visions share certain essential elements that set them apart from mere wishes or dreams. They engage all your senses. You can see, feel, taste, and touch them in your mind. They connect deeply with your values and higher purpose, ensuring that the wealth you create serves something greater than yourself. They're specific enough to feel real but expansive enough to grow as you grow. Most importantly, they create an emotional resonance that keeps you moving forward even when obstacles arise.

Where most people falter in their vision-crafting is stopping at the first level of possibility. They take their current reality and extend it forward incrementally, thinking perhaps of a better job or a bigger house. However, true visionaries understand that the first vision is rarely the boldest or most authentic one. It's often shaped by our conditioning about what's "reasonable" or "possible." The magic happens when you push past that initial boundary, asking, "What lies beyond that? And beyond that?" until you reach a vision that makes your heart race.

Thinking beyond limitations requires courage—the courage to be thought foolish, wrong, and fail publicly. It demands that you separate your vision from the "how" long enough to let yourself dream bigger than your current capabilities can support. This doesn't mean ignoring practical considerations forever; it means giving your vision room to breathe before figuring out the details. Consider the Wright brothers envisioning human flight or Alice H. Parker imagining central heating. Their visions existed before their means to achieve them.

When crafting your bold vision, think exponentially rather than linearly. Instead of asking, "What's next?" ask, "What's possible?" Rather than thinking about what you can achieve in a year, imagine what you could create in a decade if everything aligned perfectly. This isn't about being unrealistic; it's about understanding that your current definition of "realistic" is likely your greatest limitation. A truly bold vision should scare you a little and excite you a lot. It should feel like standing at the edge of a great adventure, heart pounding with equal measures of thrill and trepidation.

Your vision needs to be big enough to survive contact with reality. When the inevitable challenges arise, progress seems slow, or obstacles loom large, your vision needs to have enough gravitational pull to keep you in orbit. This is why small visions often fail; they lack the mass to maintain their hold on us when things get difficult. A bold vision, properly crafted, becomes a part of your identity. It's not just something you want to achieve; it's someone you're becoming.

Remember that your bold vision is a living thing. It should grow and evolve as you do. What seems impossibly ambitious today may feel too small tomorrow as your capacity and consciousness expand. The key is to create a vision big enough to inspire action now while leaving room for expansion as you grow into it. Think of it as writing the opening chapters of an epic story. You don't need to know every plot twist, but you need to know enough to make the journey irresistible.

Transformational Moment: The Vision Activation

Close your eyes and take a deep breath. In this moment, we're going to travel beyond the constraints of time, beyond the limitations of your current circumstances, beyond all the "buts" and "what ifs" that have held your dreams in check. This is your invitation to step into the fullness of your financial potential.

Imagine yourself five years from today, but not as a mere extension of where you are now. Instead, picture yourself in a moment of profound satisfaction, having far exceeded what your current self believes possible. Feel the weight of your body, the clothes against your skin, the air around you. Where are you? What do you see? Let the details emerge naturally, like a photograph slowly developing. Notice the quality of light, the sounds, and the textures surrounding you. This is your future, manifested exactly as your soul desires.

In this future moment, you've created wealth beyond what you once thought possible. But more than the numbers in your accounts, notice how you carry yourself differently. Feel the confidence in your posture, the ease in your movements, the peaceful certainty in your decisions about money. Observe how you think about wealth now and how naturally abundance flows through your life. This isn't just about having more—it's about becoming more.

Let your awareness expand to the impact your wealth is having on others. Who has been lifted by your success? What opportunities have you created?

What problems have you solved? Feel the profound satisfaction of knowing your financial abundance has become a force for good in the world. This is wealth with purpose, money with meaning, success that ripples outward to touch countless lives.

Now, focus on your relationship with money in this future. Notice how different it feels from your current reality. Where there was once stress, there's now ease. Where there was scarcity thinking, there's now abundant possibility. Where there was worry about the future, there's now excited anticipation. Let yourself fully inhabit this new relationship with wealth. Feel how natural it has become, like a language you now speak fluently.

Take a moment to notice the choices available to you now. Feel the freedom to say yes when your heart calls you toward something meaningful. Experience the power to make decisions based on impact rather than scarcity. Let yourself feel the joy of generosity and the thrill of investing in dreams—both yours and others. This is what true financial freedom feels like.

As you prepare to return to the present moment, know that this future version of yourself isn't just a fantasy—it's a possibility waiting to be claimed. The vision you've just experienced has planted a seed in your consciousness. Your work now is to nurture it; let it grow strong enough to pull you toward its realization. This isn't about coercion or struggle. It's about allowing yourself to be drawn naturally toward this expanded version of your life.

Take one final moment to anchor this feeling in your body. Put your hand on your heart and commit silently to this future self. Feel the alignment between who you are now and who you're becoming. Let this vision become your north star, guiding your choices and actions from this moment forward. As you open your eyes, carry with you the knowledge that this future is not just possible—it's already in motion. Your bold vision has been activated. Now, everything that follows is simply the unfolding of this new reality.

Remember this feeling. Return to it daily. Let it inform your choices, strengthen your resolve, and remind you of what's possible when you dare to dream beyond your current circumstances. This is the power of a soul-aligned vision. It doesn't just show you what's possible; it transforms who you are in the present moment, setting in motion the very changes needed to make it real.

Vision Blockers

As the glow of your vision activation begins to settle, you might notice something familiar creeping in—those persistent thoughts that have always seemed to stand between you and your boldest dreams. This is natural. In fact, it's a crucial part of the vision-building process. These voices of doubt, these whispers of limitation, aren't your enemies. They're signposts pointing directly to the beliefs that have kept your financial future small.

The most insidious of these blockers is the quiet but persistent thought: "That's not possible for someone like me." This belief often masquerades as humility or realism, but examine it closely and you'll find it's really fear wearing a sensible mask. It suggests there's a special class of people who are allowed to create extraordinary wealth, and you're not one of them. But wealth doesn't care about your background, education, or starting point. It responds to vision, action, and persistence. Every person who has created significant wealth started as "someone like you"—simply human, with dreams and doubts competing for attention.

Then there's the guilt-laden blocker: "I should be grateful for what I have." Gratitude is indeed a powerful force for attracting abundance, but it was never meant to be a ceiling on your growth. You can be deeply grateful for your current blessings while simultaneously reaching for more. In fact, the most profound gratitude often expresses itself through expansion. By expanding your capacity to receive and give, you honor the abundance you've already experienced. Think of gratitude not as contentment that keeps you small but as fertile soil from which greater possibilities can grow.

"Who am I to want more?" may be the most painful blocker of all because it questions your very worthiness to desire abundance. This voice suggests that having big financial dreams is somehow selfish or inappropriate. But consider this: Your desire for more isn't just about you. When you expand your financial capacity, you can impact the world. Your wealth can create jobs, fund solutions, support causes, and lift others. Your desire for more is actually the universe speaking through you, seeking to express more abundance through your unique gifts and vision.

The anxiety-provoking thought often lurks in the shadows: "But what will people think?" This blocker represents our deep tribal programming to stay safely within the financial norms of our social circle. We fear judgment, misunderstanding, or even rejection if we dare to break out of our economic class. Yet history shows us that every significant advancement in human prosperity came from someone willing to think differently about wealth. Your bold vision isn't an act of separation from others; it's a torch that lights the way for those who dream of more but haven't yet found the courage to admit it.

The art of transcending these blockers isn't in fighting them; resistance only makes them stronger. Instead, it's in recognizing them as outdated protection mechanisms that once served a purpose but now simply limit your expansion. When these thoughts arise, thank them for trying to keep you safe, then gently remind them that you're ready for more. Each time you choose your vision over your fears, these blockers lose a little of their power.

Think of vision blockers as weights in your mental gym. Each time you push past them, you build your vision-holding muscles. They're not obstacles to be eliminated but strengtheners to be appreciated. Your capacity to hold and manifest your bold vision grows each time you recognize a blocker and choose to expand beyond it.

Moving forward requires a new relationship with these blocking thoughts. Rather than seeing them as truth-tellers, recognize them as fear's last attempt to keep you in familiar territory. Let them become your indicators that you're pushing into new growth territory. When they arise, celebrate—you've found another opportunity to strengthen your commitment to your vision.

Remember, your vision wasn't given to you by accident. If you can see it in your mind and feel it in your heart, you can create it in reality. These blockers are simply inviting you to grow into the person who can hold and manifest that vision. As we move into crafting your vision in detail, carry this understanding with you: The presence of blockers doesn't mean you're doing something wrong—it means you're doing something revolutionary.

Crafting Your Vision

The journey from vision blocker to vision bearer begins with a single, profound choice: the decision to trust the whispers of your soul over the shouts of fear. Crafting your vision isn't merely an exercise in imagination. It's an act of courage, a declaration of possibility, and, most importantly, a commitment to becoming the person who can hold and manifest that vision.

Permission to desire is where this sacred work begins. Before you can build a vision worthy of your soul, you must first allow yourself to want what you truly want. Not what seems sensible. Not what others expect. Not even what you think you deserve. This is about connecting with your raw, unedited desires. Let yourself want outrageous things. Let yourself dream impossible dreams; the editing process can come later. For now, give your desires free rein to express themselves without judgment or limitation.

Take out your journal, find a quiet space, and let's begin this transformative process together.

Step 1: Permission to Desire. Take a deep breath and write at the top of your page: "I give myself complete permission to desire what I truly want." Then answer these questions:

> What would you want if you didn't care if people judged you?
>
> If money were infinite, how would you live?
>
> What dreams have you kept hidden, even from yourself?
>
> What would you create if success was guaranteed?

Step 2: Expanded Possibility Thinking. Look at each desire you wrote and multiply it by 10. For every goal you listed:

Why not 10 times bigger?

What would the expanded version look like?

Who else could you impact at this larger scale?

What becomes possible at this new level?

Step 3: Soul-Level Dreaming. Close your eyes and connect with your deepest truth:

What contribution do you feel called to make?

What problems light you up to solve?

Where do your gifts meet the world's needs?

What legacy do you wish to leave?

Step 4: Vision Articulation. Now, create a detailed picture of your future. Write about:

Your daily experience (Where are you? What do you see?)

Your impact (Who are you helping? What are you creating?)

Your lifestyle (How do you spend your time? What choices do you make?)

Your relationships (How do you interact with others? Who surrounds you?)

Your resources (What opportunities can you say yes to? How do you use your wealth?)

Step 5: Emotional Connection Feel into your vision physically:

Place your hand on your heart

Read your vision aloud

Circle the parts that make you feel excited or scared

Note the sensations in your body as you connect with each aspect

Give yourself permission to feel the full magnitude of your desires

Vision Refinement Questions: After completing each step, ask yourself:

> Does this vision make my heart race?
>
> Is it big enough to pull me forward?
>
> Does it serve something greater than myself?
>
> Can I feel it in my body?
>
> Does it scare me a little?

Daily Vision Practice:

> Read your vision every morning
>
> Visualize one aspect in detail
>
> Feel the emotions of already having achieved it
>
> Take one action aligned with your vision
>
> Journal about new possibilities as they emerge

Remember, your vision is a living document. Return to these steps regularly, allowing your vision to expand as you do. Let each success inform a bigger dream, each setback clarify your resolve, and each day bring you closer to the future you're creating.

Wealth Wisdom Note: The most powerful visions are those that scare and excite you in equal measure. If your vision feels completely comfortable, revisit Step 2 and dare to dream bigger.

Vision Activation Commitment: Complete this exercise by writing: "I commit to becoming the person who can hold and manifest this vision. I choose to let this future pull me forward, knowing that each step I take shapes the reality I'm creating."

This is not a one-time exercise but a living practice. Return to these steps whenever you feel your vision needs refreshing or expansion. Your capacity to hold and manifest wealth will grow with each iteration.

What surprised you most about your vision? What part makes you most uncomfortable? These are often the areas ripe for the greatest growth and transformation.

From Vision To Reality

The gap between vision and reality is bridged not by one giant leap but through a series of intentional steps, each building upon the last. This journey from ethereal dream to tangible reality requires both the soaring spirit of your vision and the grounded wisdom of practical action. In this sacred space between dreaming and doing, your future takes shape.

Creating milestone markers serves as your compass on this journey. Rather than focusing solely on your magnificent end vision, break it down into meaningful markers that signal your progress. Think of these as base camps on your climb to the summit. Each milestone should be significant enough to celebrate but achievable enough to maintain momentum. These aren't just financial targets—they're markers of your expanding capacity, growing impact, and evolving identity as a steward of wealth.

Building belief bridges is perhaps the most crucial element of this journey. Your current beliefs can only sustain your current reality. To create something bigger, you must consciously construct new beliefs to hold your expanding vision. Start by identifying the gap between your current beliefs about wealth and the beliefs needed to manifest your vision. Then, create intermediate beliefs that help you cross this gap. If believing in a million-dollar business feels impossible, start by believing you can double your current income. Each success strengthens your belief bridge, making the next expansion more accessible.

Taking inspired action differentiates dreams from destiny. Inspired action flows from your vision rather than from obligation or fear. Each morning, ask yourself, "What action aligns most with my vision today?" Sometimes, this action will be practical—making that bold phone call, investing in a financial coach, or having that crucial conversation. Other times, it will be energetic—

carrying yourself with the confidence of your future self, making decisions from abundance rather than scarcity, or treating your current resources as seeds of future wealth.

Maintaining vision momentum requires a delicate balance between patience and persistence. There will be days when your vision feels distant, doubt creeps in, and the gap between where you are and where you're going feels impossibly wide. These moments don't signal failure. They're opportunities to deepen your commitment, strengthen your belief muscles, and refine your strategies. Vision momentum isn't about constant forward motion; it's about maintaining your connection to possibility even when progress feels slow.

The key to sustainable progress lies in celebrating every step forward, no matter how small. Each aligned action, expanded belief, and milestone reached is evidence of your vision taking form. Create rituals of acknowledgment that honor your progress while strengthening your resolve for the journey ahead. These celebrations aren't about reaching the destination—they're about becoming the person who can hold and manifest your boldest dreams.

Remember that the path from vision to reality is rarely linear. There will be unexpected detours, surprising shortcuts, and moments of quantum leaps forward. Stay flexible in your methods while remaining steadfast in your commitment; your vision knows the way. Your job is to stay open to guidance while taking consistent action in the right direction.

As you move forward, ask yourself: "Who am I becoming through this process?" The greatest transformation happens not in your external circumstances but in your internal capacity to hold and steward wealth. Each challenge you face, each fear you move through, and each success you create sculpts you into someone who can naturally attract and maintain greater levels of abundance.

Let your vision pull you forward rather than pushing yourself toward it. This subtle shift from forcing to allowing, from striving to aligning, makes the journey more effective and enjoyable. Your vision isn't just about reaching a destination—it's about experiencing the joy of becoming more fully yourself with each step forward.

Trust that every aligned action, no matter how small, contains the seeds of your vision's fulfillment within it. Like an artist bringing forth a masterpiece, you're creating your future through daily choices and actions that gradually transform possibility into reality. The bridge from vision to reality is built one choice at a time, one action at a time, one celebration at a time. Keep your vision clear, your actions aligned, and your heart open to the magic that unfolds when you dare to bring your boldest dreams to life.

Remember, the journey from vision to reality is a form of wealth—rich with learning, growth, and transformation. Embrace each step, knowing that you're not just creating a financial future; you're becoming the person your soul knows you're meant to be.

Wealth Wisdom Reflection:
1. What financial future would thrill you?
2. Where are you playing too small?
3. What becomes possible when you succeed?
4. Who else benefits from your bold vision?

From Welfare To Wealth With A Vision

In 1994, Lisa Nichols found herself in a moment that would either break her spirit or become the catalyst for an extraordinary vision. As a single mother with less than $12 in her bank account, using public assistance to feed her young son, and wrapping towels around her baby when she couldn't afford diapers, Lisa faced a reality that many would consider insurmountable. But in that moment of profound scarcity, she made a decision that would alter not just her destiny but the lives of millions.

Her vision began not with dreams of wealth or fame but with a simple yet powerful commitment: Her son would never have to live through the struggle she was experiencing. This initial spark of determination, born from necessity, would gradually expand into a vision encompassing far more than financial security. Lisa began to see herself as more than her circumstances. She saw herself as a messenger, a transformer, a catalyst for change in others' lives.

The path forward wasn't smooth or straight. Lisa worked multiple jobs while studying successful speakers and authors, investing what little money she had in personal development books and programs. She practiced speaking in front of her bathroom mirror, imagining audiences being transformed by her words even as she struggled to keep the electricity on. Her vision sustained her through countless rejections, moments when giving up seemed like the logical choice, and times when her bank account didn't match the future she saw so clearly in her mind.

What set Lisa's journey apart wasn't just her persistence—it was her extraordinary ability to maintain a bold vision while taking humble steps forward. She started small, speaking at schools and community centers, often for free. Each presentation, regardless of the size of the audience, was delivered with the same passion and commitment she would later bring to international stages. She understood that her present reality was simply the launching pad for her vision, not the predictor of her future.

As her expertise grew, so did her impact. Her speaking business began to flourish, leading to opportunities with transformational programs and books. Her appearance in "The Secret" expanded her reach globally, but Lisa never lost sight of her core vision: to serve others by showing them what's possible when you dare to dream beyond your circumstances. Her company, Motivating the Masses, became one of the largest transformation companies in the world, but more importantly, it became a vehicle for creating generational impact.

At the time of this writing, Lisa is preparing for her Broadway debut with "*When My Soul Speaks*." She embodies the power of an ever-expanding vision. From that young mother on welfare to a multi-millionaire transformational speaker preparing to share her story on Broadway's prestigious stage, her journey demonstrates how a vision, held with unwavering faith and backed by consistent action, can exceed even the wildest dreams.

What makes Lisa's story particularly powerful is her willingness to continue expanding her vision. Even after achieving levels of success that would satisfy most people, she continues to ask, "What else is possible?" Her upcoming Broadway show (which I am honored to be an executive producer of) will share never-before-told stories from her "double and triple vault," representing her commitment to perpetual growth and impact.

Lisa's wealth-creation journey wasn't just about accumulating money but about becoming someone who could impact millions while creating opportunities for others. Her vision expanded from feeding her son to feeding souls worldwide, from wrapping her baby in towels to wrapping thousands in transformational experiences that change their lives forever.

Through her story, we learn that a bold vision isn't just about seeing a bigger future; it's about becoming the person who can hold and manifest that future. Lisa's journey from welfare to wealth, from survival to significance, from public assistance to public inspiration reminds us that our current circumstances are merely the starting point of our story, never the end.

As Lisa steps onto the Broadway stage in 2024, she continues to demonstrate that when we dare to hold a vision bigger than our current reality—and back it with unwavering faith and consistent action—we become living proof of what's possible. Her story isn't just about personal transformation; it's about the ripple effect that occurs when one person refuses to let their past dictate their future, choosing instead to let their vision guide them toward extraordinary impact.

Sustaining Your Vision

The journey from vision to manifestation isn't a straight line but a spiral path that often revisits familiar territories of doubt, challenge, and renewed commitment. Understanding how to sustain your vision through these natural cycles becomes as crucial as the vision itself. This is where the real work of wealth creation happens—not in the moments of inspiration, but in the daily choice to keep believing when reality hasn't yet caught up to your dreams.

Doubt phases are not your enemy but rather natural checkpoints in your growth. Like a muscle being stretched, your capacity to hold a bigger vision occasionally needs to contract before it can expand further. When doubt arises, treat it as a signal that you're pushing beyond your comfort zone. Rather than fighting these phases, learn to move through them with grace. Ask yourself: "What is this doubt trying to teach me? What part of me needs strengthening to hold this next level of possibility?" Sometimes, doubt simply indicates that your vision needs more clarity or that your "why" needs deepening.

Navigating setbacks requires a fundamental reframing of your thought process. Every apparent obstacle is actually an opportunity to strengthen your vision-holding capacity. When things don't go as planned—when investments fall short, opportunities dissolve, or progress seems to reverse—resist the temptation to make these moments mean anything about your vision's validity. Instead, view setbacks as reality's way of helping you build the foundation needed for sustainable success. Each challenge overcome becomes a story of resilience in your wealth creation journey.

The art of strengthening belief lies in consistent, intentional practice. Just as you would exercise a physical muscle, your belief system needs regular workouts to maintain and increase its capacity to hold your vision. Start each day by reconnecting with your vision through visualization. Surround yourself with evidence of possibility: stories of others who've achieved similar dreams, proof of your past successes, and signs of progress, no matter how small. Create a "belief book" where you document every win, every synchronicity, every step forward, building a personal reference library of possibility.

Celebrating progress becomes your secret weapon in vision sustainability. Most people wait for the big wins to celebrate, missing countless opportunities to strengthen their belief muscles through acknowledging smaller victories. Develop the habit of celebrating everything—the inspired actions you take, the fears you move through, the boundaries you set, and the new thoughts you choose. Each celebration anchors your vision more deeply into your neural pathways, making it increasingly natural to hold and manifest bigger possibilities.

Remember that vision maintenance is as important as vision creation. Schedule regular vision renewal sessions—weekly, monthly, and quarterly—to revisit, refine, and recommit to your bold future. Use these sessions to clear any doubts, update your action plans, and strengthen your connection to your vision; nurture your vision like a precious garden, giving it the regular attention it needs to flourish.

Your relationship with time becomes crucial to sustaining your vision. While urgency can be a powerful motivator, it can also breed disappointment when things take longer than expected. Develop a long-term perspective that allows for divine timing while maintaining steady progress. Think in terms of seasons rather than days, years rather than months. This temporal expansion helps you stay committed while remaining flexible about the exact path to manifestation.

Build a vision support system of people and practices that help you maintain your connection to possibility. This might include mentors who've walked similar paths, peers who share your commitment to growth, or a Neuro-transformational Life and Money Coach such as myself who can guide specific aspects of your wealth creation journey. Regular engagement with this support system helps normalize your bold vision and provides perspective when challenges arise.

Develop a personal resilience practice that helps you bounce back from setbacks more quickly. This might include meditation, journaling, movement, or any activity that helps you return to a state of possibility. The goal isn't to avoid difficulties but to move through them with increasing grace and speed, maintaining your vision even when the path forward isn't clear.

Every sustained vision requires ongoing renewal of your commitment to its manifestation. This isn't a one-time decision but a series of choices made daily, sometimes hourly, to align your thoughts, feelings, and actions with your desired future. Let each choice strengthen your resolve, each setback deepen your commitment, and each celebration affirm your path.

Remember that sustaining your vision is ultimately about becoming the person who can hold and manifest it naturally. This transformation happens gradually, through consistent choice and practice, until your bold vision feels less like a distant dream and more like an inevitable unfolding of who you're becoming.

Your vision isn't just about numbers in a bank account; it's about who you become in pursuit of it. As you strengthen this vision, you'll make different choices, take bolder actions, and create bigger results. In the next chapter, we'll explore how to turn this vision into empowered action, but first, take a moment to dream. What bold vision is your soul ready to claim?

KEY TAKEAWAYS:
- Vision differs from goals in depth and power
- Bold visions pull you toward greater possibilities
- Vision blockers can limit financial expansion
- Your vision shapes your financial reality

PART 3: LIVING YOUR TRUTH

CHAPTER 7

From Vision To Victory

Sitting in my tiny sublet room, surrounded by carefully curated pictures of my dream home, I faced a hard truth. Every room I'd imagined—from the sun-drenched kitchen to the spacious primary bedroom—was beautifully planned and perfectly detailed. But no amount of visualization or manifestation was going to turn those pictures into reality—not without action.

The gap between my current reality and my dream home seemed impossibly wide. My credit score of 547 felt like a locked door between me and homeownership, and my living space was barely big enough to contain my dreams, let alone bring them to life. But in that small room, on my lopsided air mattress, I decided to change everything. Instead of just dreaming about my future home, I would build the foundation to make it possible.

I threw myself into understanding credit with the same intensity I'd put into choosing every detail of my future home. I researched credit utilization ratios, payment histories, and credit mix late into the night and on off days. But unlike my previous pattern of endless research without action, each piece of knowledge became a stepping stone to concrete moves this time. I applied for credit cards strategically. I watched my utilization rates like a hawk. Every payment was made with meticulous precision.

The progress was painfully slow at first. When my score crept up to 589, it felt like watching paint dry. The jump to 611 came after months of consistent, careful action. There were moments of frustration when the numbers seemed stuck, times when I questioned if all this effort would really lead to my future home. But I kept going, understanding that each small action was laying another brick in the foundation of my future.

Many don't realize that the journey from dreaming to doing is not about one giant leap—it's about thousands of tiny, consistent choices. It's about making every payment on time, even when emergencies arise. It's about resisting the urge to spend, even when tempting opportunities arise. It's about staying focused on the long game when everything around you demands immediate gratification.

Two years later, I sat across from a mortgage broker, my heart pounding as he reviewed my application. I almost fainted when he looked up and told me my median credit score was 702, qualifying me for a 3.5% interest rate. Every small action had led to that moment. The future home I'd so carefully visualized years ago wasn't just pictures I gathered from the internet—it was about to become reality.

Knowledge isn't the gap between you and your financial dreams. Action is.

Think about it; you probably know more about money management than 90% of people from a generation ago. You even have access to investment information that used to be reserved for the financial elite. You've likely read books, attended workshops, and maybe even hired coaches.

Yet, knowing and doing are different currencies. It's in the doing that wealth is built.

Beyond The Wisdom Hoarding

In today's digital age, we've become masters of information collection but novices at implementation. It's seductively easy to convince ourselves that one more book, course, or certification will finally bridge the gap between where we are and where we want to be financially. This pattern of perpetual preparation has become a comfortable substitute for the uncomfortable reality of taking action.

Information hoarding has become a sophisticated form of procrastination. Each new piece of financial knowledge provides a temporary hit of accomplishment, making us feel like we're progressing toward our goals when we're actually standing still. We gather financial information like collectors' items, storing it away for that mythical "perfect moment" when we'll finally feel ready to act.

This cycle creates what I call the "knowledge comfort zone"—a place where we feel safe in our expertise but remain untested in real-world applications. The cost of this perpetual preparation isn't just measured in time lost; it's calculated in unrealized gains, unmade investments, and untapped potential. Every month spent studying another strategy instead of implementing what you already know is another month your money isn't growing, your business isn't scaling up, and your financial goals aren't materializing.

Breaking free from this learning loop requires a fundamental shift in perspective. The goal isn't to stop learning; continuous education remains vital in our ever-evolving financial landscape. Instead, the key is to transform your relationship with knowledge, seeing it not as a prerequisite for action but as a companion to it. True financial wisdom emerges not from what you know but from what you implement.

The path forward lies in recognizing that imperfect action always trumps perfect knowledge. Your financial journey doesn't require mastery of every concept before beginning; it demands the courage to start with what you know now. The most successful individuals in any field aren't those who know the most—they're those who act the most effectively on what they know.

Consider that many of the experts you admire started with less knowledge than you have right now. They didn't wait until they had all the answers; they moved forward with what they knew, learning and adjusting along the way. This is the essence of growing wealth; it's not in the theoretical realm of endless preparation but in the practical world of consistent action.

The Anatomy of Empowered Action

Understanding the difference between busy work and power moves is crucial in your financial journey. Busy work often masquerades as progress—checking your investment accounts multiple times daily, endlessly comparing credit card rewards programs, or reorganizing your budget spreadsheets for the tenth time. While these activities feel productive, they rarely move the needle on your wealth-building goals. Power moves, on the other hand, are decisive actions that create measurable forward momentum—opening that investment account you've been researching for months, having the difficult conversation about rates with your biggest client, or finally setting up your automated savings system.

The components of confident action aren't what most people expect. They don't require unwavering certainty or the complete absence of fear. Instead, they're built on three core elements: clarity of intention, acceptance of imperfection, and commitment to movement. Clarity helps you identify which actions will create the most significant impact. Acceptance allows you to move forward despite inevitable uncertainties. Commitment keeps you going when initial enthusiasm fades.

Most people get stuck in what I call the "preparation paralysis zone." This is where fear disguises itself as prudence and overthinking poses as thoroughness. You might recognize this pattern if you've ever found yourself saying, "I just need to research one more thing," or "I'll start once I have a perfect plan." The truth is, this zone is less about preparation and more about protecting ourselves from the discomfort of potential failure or judgment.

Moving through fear requires understanding that it's not an obstacle to action; it's a natural part of the growth process. The most successful wealth builders aren't fearless; they're fear-fluent. They've learned to interpret anxiety about money moves as a signal that they're pushing their comfort zone, not a warning to retreat. This shift in perspective transforms fear from a stop sign into a growth indicator.

The secret lies in recognizing that confidence isn't a prerequisite for action—it's a result of it. Each time you take a bold financial step, whether it succeeds or not, you build what I call your "action resilience." This is the deep-seated knowledge that you can handle whatever comes your way, not because you've planned for every possibility, but because you've proven to yourself that you can navigate uncertainty.

Think of each power move as a deposit in your confidence bank account. Just as compound interest grows your wealth over time, compound action grows your capability and courage. The key is starting where you are, with what you have, and taking steps that stretch you without breaking you. Every successful wealth journey is built on this foundation of consistent, intentional action, even (and especially) in the face of uncertainty.

Transformational Moment: The Action Activation

Take a deep breath and settle into this moment. We're about to move beyond theory into real, tangible action that will begin shifting your financial trajectory right now. Find a quiet space where you can focus fully on this exercise. Grab a pen and paper. This isn't just another reading exercise; it's your launching pad for transformation.

Start by identifying three financial decisions or actions you've been postponing. Write them down without censoring yourself. These might be small moves like setting up that retirement account or bigger leaps like investing in real estate or starting your side business. Now, pause and notice the physical sensations that arise as you review your list. That flutter in your stomach? The tightness in your chest? These are normal responses to stretching beyond your comfort zone. Welcome them as signs that you're on the right track.

Next, we will break through the paralysis by focusing on just one power move. Look at your list and ask yourself: "Which of these actions, if taken, would create the most meaningful shift in my financial life?" Circle that item. This is your focal point—your next power move. Now, here's where most people stop, overwhelmed by the magnitude of their chosen action. But we're going to do something different.

Take your power move and break it down into its smallest possible component—something so simple it would be almost impossible not to do it. If your power move is "Start investing in stocks," your micro-move might be "Open my browser and search brokerage firms." If it's "Create a side business," your micro-move could be "Write down three skills I could monetize." The key is making the first step so small that it bypasses your brain's fear response.

Here's the transformational part: Right now—yes, in this very moment— make that micro-move. Don't close this book and promise to do it later. Don't wait for the perfect time. The perfect time is now while you're in this energy of possibility. Take that tiny action that begins breaking the pattern of postponement.

Feel the shift that happens when you move from thinking about action to taking action. Notice how your energy changes and how possibility opens up. This is the power of activated momentum. Your small step forward has just created a crack in the wall of inaction, and light is streaming in through that crack.

Now, riding this wave of activated energy, schedule your next micro-move for tomorrow. Make it specific, make it small, but most importantly, make it non-negotiable. You're not just planning anymore; you're building a bridge from where you are to where you want to be, one plank at a time.

This is how transformation happens—not in grand gestures, but in conscious, consistent choices to move forward despite uncertainty. You've just taken your first step. The momentum is building. Can you feel it?

Action Blockers

Let's face the familiar voices that keep us stuck in financial inaction, not by fighting them, but by understanding and transforming them. These mental blocks aren't character flaws; they're protective mechanisms that have outlived their usefulness. By recognizing them, we can consciously choose a different response.

"I need to learn more first" is perhaps the most insidious of all action blockers. It sounds responsible, even admirable. After all, shouldn't we be well-informed before making financial decisions? But this blocker often masks a deeper fear of responsibility. When you catch yourself saying this, ask: "What's the minimum information I truly need to take the next small step?" Usually, you'll find you already have more than enough knowledge to begin. Remember, experience is the most powerful teacher. You'll learn more from taking imperfect action than from reading another dozen articles about what you should do.

"What if I make a mistake?" reveals our perfectionist tendencies and our binary thinking about success and failure. The reality is every successful investor, entrepreneur, and wealth builder has made countless mistakes. These weren't setbacks—they were feedback loops that refined their approach. Instead of seeing mistakes as failures to avoid, reframe them as investments in your financial education. The cost of a mistake is finite; the cost of perpetual inaction is infinite. Besides, in most cases, financial mistakes can be corrected or adjusted. The bigger mistake is letting fear keep you stuck.

"I'm not ready yet" is often code for "I don't feel worthy" or "I don't trust myself." This blocker stems from the misconception that readiness is a feeling rather than a choice. The truth is readiness is a decision, not an emotion. The most successful people in the world often report not feeling ready when they take their biggest steps forward. They simply decided that the cost of waiting exceeded the discomfort of action. Your sense of readiness will follow your actions, not precede them.

"The timing isn't perfect" is perhaps the most deceptive blocker because it seems logical. We tell ourselves we'll invest when the market conditions are ideal, start our business when the economy is better, or save more when we make more money. But perfect timing is a myth. The best time to plant a tree was twenty years ago; the second-best time is now. The same principle applies to your financial growth. While timing matters, waiting for perfect conditions often means missing opportunities entirely. Success comes from learning to act decisively in imperfect conditions.

The key to moving past these blockers isn't to eliminate them—it's to act alongside them. Acknowledge their presence and understand their protective intent, but don't let them drive your decisions. Instead of waiting for these voices to quiet down, learn to take action while they're still speaking. This is the essence of financial courage: not the absence of fear or doubt, but the willingness to move forward despite them.

Creating Your Action Plan

A strategic framework that turns your financial vision into tangible steps closes the gap between intention and action. This isn't about creating another to-do list—it's about engineering a pathway that aligns with your goals and natural tendencies for action.

Let these inquiries lead you to your most potent action steps.

1. Identifying Your Power Moves

    Which actions would create the biggest positive impact on your financial life right now?

    What three financial decisions, if made today, would significantly change your trajectory?

    Where are you playing small when you could be making bigger moves?

    What financial action, if taken consistently, would transform your wealth over the next year?

    Which move would open the most doors for future opportunities?

2. Understanding Your Barriers

    What specifically stops you each time you attempt to take financial action?

    When you think about your biggest financial move, what fear comes up first?

    Who do you need in your corner to help you push through resistance?

What resources would make your next step feel more manageable?

How can you prepare now for the challenges you expect to face?

3. Designing Your Success Systems

    What daily money habits would best support your financial growth?

    How could you reorganize your schedule to prioritize financial actions?

    Which current habits could you piggyback your new financial practices onto?

    What would your ideal weekly money management routine look like?

    How can you automate your most important financial decisions?

4. Creating Momentum

    What small win could you achieve this week to build confidence?

    How will you track your progress in a way that motivates you?

    Which successful habit could you expand or build upon?

    What would make taking consistent action easier for you?

    How will you maintain enthusiasm when initial excitement fades?

5. Acknowledging Progress

    How will you celebrate completing each power move?

    Who will you share your financial wins with?

    What evidence of progress will you document?

    How will you use your successes to fuel future actions?

    What rewards would motivate you to maintain momentum?

Implementation Questions:

Daily Reflection:

What's the one financial power move I commit to today?

When is my peak energy time to tackle this action?

How will I track this move's impact on my larger goals?

Weekly Planning:

>What did I learn from last week's actions?

>Which moves created the most significant results?

>How can I build on these successes next week?

Monthly Review:

>What patterns am I noticing in my financial actions?

>Where do I see the biggest returns on my efforts?

>What adjustments would make my action plan more effective?

>What new targets would stretch me appropriately?

Remember, these questions aren't meant to be answered all at once. Choose the ones that resonate most strongly with your current situation and use them as starting points for deeper exploration. Your answers will evolve as you grow in your financial journey.

Sustainable Success Systems

Building lasting financial transformation isn't about grand gestures or sporadic bursts of motivation; it's about creating a foundation of reliable systems that carry you forward even when inspiration wanes. These systems become the invisible architecture of your wealth-building journey, supporting consistent progress through challenges and victories.

Creating empowered habits begins with aligning your financial practices with your natural rhythms and tendencies. Observe when you're most clear-headed about money decisions rather than forcing yourself into someone else's ideal routine. Notice which times of day you have the most emotional and mental bandwidth for financial tasks. Then, design your habits to flow with these natural patterns. This might mean reviewing your investments first thing in the morning when your mind is fresh or scheduling important money conversations for early evening when you feel most grounded.

Building wealth routines requires a delicate balance between structure and flexibility. Start by identifying your non-negotiable financial practices—those actions that must happen regardless of circumstances. These might include daily expense tracking, weekly budget reviews, or monthly investment evaluations. Then, create clear protocols for each routine, making them specific enough to follow easily but flexible enough to adapt when life throws inevitable curveballs. The key is establishing rhythms that feel sustainable rather than restrictive.

Accountability structures serve as the scaffolding for your financial growth. They aren't just about having someone check your progress—they're about creating a comprehensive support system that keeps you aligned with your goals. This includes internal accountability measures, like tracking systems and personal check-ins, as well as external support through mentors, accountability partners, or financial advisors. The most effective structures combine regular monitoring with opportunities for adjustment and growth.

Maintaining momentum becomes possible when your systems are designed to work together harmoniously. Think of your financial systems as an ecosystem where each element supports the others. Your daily habits feed into your weekly routines, which inform your monthly reviews and guide your quarterly planning. This interconnected approach ensures that progress in one area naturally reinforces growth in others.

The real power of sustainable systems lies in their ability to automate beneficial behaviors while still keeping you actively engaged in your financial journey. It's about creating what I call "conscious automation"—where the basic foundations of your financial life happen automatically, freeing your mental energy for higher-level strategic decisions. This might look like automatic savings transfers combined with monthly investment strategy reviews or scheduled bill payments paired with quarterly spending analysis sessions.

Remember that sustainable systems grow and evolve with you. What works in the early stages of your financial journey may need refinement as your wealth and complexity increase. Regular system audits help you identify what's working, what needs adjustment, and what new structures might better serve your current reality. The goal isn't perfection but progress—creating systems resilient enough to support your growth while remaining flexible enough to adapt as you evolve.

The Confidence Compound Effect

Just as compound interest transforms modest investments into significant wealth over time, compound confidence turns small actions into unshakeable financial self-trust. Each time you follow through on a money commitment, make a bold financial decision or navigate a challenging monetary situation, you're not just affecting your bank account – you're building your confidence capital.

This compound effect begins with what might seem like insignificant choices. Perhaps you finally make that call to set up your retirement account, negotiate a raise for the first time, or have an honest conversation about money with your partner. In isolation, these actions might appear small. But just like compound interest, the real magic lies in the accumulation and acceleration of these choices over time.

The momentum builds slowly at first, so slowly you might question if anything is really changing. But beneath the surface, something powerful is happening. Each action, regardless of its outcome, deposits evidence into what I call your "confidence bank." When you need to make bigger financial decisions later, you can draw on this accumulated evidence of your capability. You begin to trust yourself more deeply because you have a proven track record of taking action, learning from results, and moving forward regardless of circumstances.

Breaking through plateaus becomes easier as your confidence compounds. Where you once hesitated to invest a few hundred dollars, you now confidently manage thousands. Decisions that used to keep you awake at night become manageable challenges you know you can handle. This isn't because the decisions themselves have become easier; it's because your capacity to handle them has grown through the compound effect of consistent action.

Your growth accelerates as this confidence compounds. You begin taking actions that would have seemed impossible in the early stages of your journey. More importantly, you start recovering from setbacks more quickly. A market downturn that might have once sent you into a panic becomes an opportunity you know how to navigate. A financial miscalculation that would have previously derailed you for weeks becomes a learning experience you can integrate and move forward from.

This compounds not just your confidence but your actual financial results. Because you trust yourself more, you're willing to seize opportunities faster. Because you've built evidence of your resilience, you're able to take calculated risks that others might shy away from. Each success builds upon the last, creating an upward spiral of both internal confidence and external results.

The key is understanding that this compound effect works in both directions. Just as consistent action builds confidence over time, consistent inaction or avoidance can compound doubt and hesitation. This is why starting small—but starting now—is so crucial. Every day you take action, no matter how modest, you're investing in your confidence compound effect. Every day you choose movement over paralysis, you're building the foundation for bigger moves to come.

Wealth Wisdom Reflection:

1. What action have you been avoiding?

2. Where are you over-preparing?

3. What's your next power move?

4. Who are you becoming through action?

From Overwhelm to Empowered Action

"I know what I need to do," Angie told me during our first meeting, her voice heavy with frustration. "I need a budget, I need to fix my credit, I need to get out of debt. But knowing what to do and actually doing it feel like two completely different things." Like so many others, Angie had found herself caught in the gap between financial knowledge and financial action. Her dream of owning a vehicle—and the freedom it represented—seemed to be slipping further away the more she learned about what it would take to get there.

The weight of everything she needed to do had created a paralysis that kept her stuck. Each piece of financial advice she collected, rather than empowering her, had become another boulder in an increasingly overwhelming mountain of "shoulds." When she reached out to me, her words captured the frustration of information without implementation, "I know I got to do better with my money... but I just feel so stuck. All of this feels like it's just too much, especially with this debt."

I invited her to take a deep breath—a simple but powerful action that would become symbolic of her journey from overwhelmed to empowered. "You tackle this problem just like you would any other problem," I told her, "piece by piece. Because no matter how hard you try, you couldn't do everything all at once anyway." This became our mantra as we broke down her financial transformation into discrete, manageable power moves.

Each week, we focused on just one action item. Instead of trying to overhaul her entire financial life at once, Angie learned to trust the compound effect of consistent, focused action. One week, she tracked her spending without judgment; the next, she negotiated with a single creditor. Step by step, she moved from knowing what she should do to actually doing it.

The transformation wasn't just in her numbers—though those certainly improved. Her debt began to decrease, her credit score started climbing, and her spending plan evolved from a theoretical budget into a practical tool that supported her goals. But the real shift happened in her relationship with financial action itself. What had once felt overwhelming became a series of manageable steps. Each small success supported her growing financial confidence.

Three months into our work together, Angie shared a revelation: "I used to think I needed to feel ready or confident before I could take action. Now I realize that taking action is what creates the confidence." This insight became the cornerstone of her continued growth. Instead of waiting to feel prepared, she learned to let her actions lead the way.

Today, Angie's financial life looks radically different—not because she gained more knowledge, but because she learned to turn knowledge into consistent action. Her story reminds us that financial transformation doesn't require grandiose moves or perfect plans. It requires the courage to take one step, then another, and another, letting each action build momentum for the next.

Mastering Momentum

The journey to financial mastery isn't a straight line. It's a series of cycles, each building upon the last to create unstoppable forward motion. Understanding how to maintain and harness this momentum, especially through inevitable challenges, becomes the cornerstone of lasting financial success. This isn't about avoiding setbacks but transforming them into stepping stones for stronger advancement.

Handling setbacks requires a fundamental shift in perspective. When market conditions fluctuate, investment returns disappoint, or business ventures don't meet expectations, these aren't failures; they're feedback loops rich with information. The key lies in developing what I call "resilient responsiveness"— the ability to absorb the lesson without absorbing the doubt. Each setback contains within it the seeds of a stronger strategy, but only if we're willing to look past the immediate disappointment to find the deeper wisdom.

Adjusting strategies becomes an art form in itself. Too often, we either abandon our approach at the first sign of trouble or stick rigidly to plans that no longer serve us. The sweet spot lies in what I call "flexible persistence." That is, maintaining your core financial principles while adapting your tactical approach based on real-world results. This might mean adjusting your investment allocation without abandoning your long-term investment philosophy or modifying your savings strategy while keeping your wealth-building goals intact.

Building resilience in your financial journey isn't about becoming harder or more stringent—it's about developing greater flexibility and deeper trust in your ability to navigate change. This resilience grows through what I call "progressive challenge"—intentionally taking on slightly bigger financial moves as your confidence and capability expands. Each successful navigation of a challenging situation becomes evidence of your growing capacity to handle whatever comes next.

Celebrating wins becomes a pleasant addition, and a strategic necessity, to maintaining momentum. Too often, we rush past our successes in our hurry to reach the next goal. However, conscious celebration serves a crucial function; it anchors the positive emotions of achievement into our neural pathways, making future action more likely and more natural. This doesn't mean waiting for massive victories. Even small wins, when properly acknowledged, build the emotional foundation for bigger successes.

The most powerful momentum comes from what I call "integrated acceleration," where each aspect of your financial life builds upon and reinforces the others. Your investment success feeds your business confidence, which strengthens your ability to set healthy money boundaries, which in turn supports better investment decisions. This creates a self-reinforcing cycle of growth and expansion that becomes increasingly resilient to external challenges.

Remember, mastering momentum isn't about maintaining constant forward motion; it's about understanding the natural rhythm of progress. There will be times of intense acceleration and times of apparent stillness. The key is recognizing that you're building potential energy for your next leap forward, even during quiet periods. Trust the process, maintain your practices, and keep your vision clear. The momentum will carry you forward, one conscious choice at a time.

Your actions write your financial future, one move at a time. Throughout this chapter, we've explored the profound difference between knowing and doing, between collecting information and creating transformation.

The greatest gap between you and your financial dreams isn't knowledge—it's action. This gap is starkly illustrated by the National Endowment for Financial Education's 2023 findings that only 40% of Americans who know they need to save for retirement actually take action to do so. However, there's hope in structure. A 2023 Financial Health Network study shows that people who implement automated savings systems save 53% more than those who don't. The difference isn't in knowing more; it's in doing more. More importantly, you've discovered that this gap isn't bridged through grand gestures but through consistent, courageous steps forward.

As you strengthen your action muscle, you'll find yourself moving with increasing confidence. What once seemed daunting becomes doable. Decisions that used to paralyze you become manageable challenges. This isn't because the financial landscape has changed—it's because you have. Each power move you make, each system you implement, and each moment of choosing action over analysis builds your capacity for bigger moves to come.

Creating bigger results becomes inevitable when you combine clear intention with consistent action. Your financial growth accelerates not through perfect choices but through persistent movement. Like a river finding its path to the ocean, your journey may take unexpected turns, but your consistent forward motion ensures you'll reach your destination. The momentum you're building now becomes the foundation for every financial victory in your future.

In the next chapter, we'll explore how to integrate these actions into a sustainable lifestyle—one that supports not just your financial growth but your overall well-being. We'll discover how to create harmony between your wealth-building journey and broader life aspirations. But first, take a moment to commit to yourself. What empowered action is ready to emerge through you? What power move will you make today that your future self will thank you for?

Remember, your financial future isn't shaped by what you know but by what you do. The perfect moment for action isn't coming; it's already here. Let your next move be one of power, purpose, and possibility. Your journey to financial abundance isn't waiting for more information; it's waiting for your next decisive step forward.

KEY TAKEAWAYS:
- Action bridges the gap between vision and reality
- Knowledge without implementation creates stagnation
- Small consistent actions create major transformation
- Empowered action builds lasting results

CHAPTER 8

Living Your Wealth Truth

The city sprawls before me as I sit on my back porch, taking in the view that reminds me daily of how far I've come in my relationship with wealth. I must confess it took me a while to fully accept that I could be wealthy. Like many others, I, too, had fallen for the notion that wanting more was excessive and there was no need to have so much more than I needed.

The journey to this understanding wasn't linear. I remember countless mornings like this one, sitting here wrestling with the internal conflict between my growing success and the deeply ingrained beliefs about money that had shaped my early life. The city lights served as a metaphor for my own awakening—each glow representing a different perspective on what wealth could mean.

As I got deeper into the financial and spiritual worlds, something profound shifted. I realized that wealth is about more than just money and luxury–wealth is about the freedom to live life on your own terms. This porch, overlooking the cityscape, became my thinking spot, my place of integration, where I could see how all the pieces of my life—financial success, personal fulfillment, and spiritual growth—could coexist beautifully.

Now, each morning I spend here reinforces that truth. The view reminds me that wealth isn't about reaching a destination but expanding our vision of what's possible. Just as the city contains countless paths and possibilities,

I've learned that there are infinite ways to express and experience abundance while staying true to who you are.

The transformation from seeing wealth as something external to recognizing it as an internal state of being has changed everything about how I live and work. Now, when I share this perspective with others, I often invite them to shift their own mindset—to see wealth not as something to chase but as something to embody, not as something to achieve but as something to become.

This moment, right here on my porch, overlooking the life I've created, stands as a testament to what's possible when we release our limiting beliefs about wealth and allow ourselves to expand into our full potential. The journey continues to unfold, but now it does so from a place of integration rather than separation, from acceptance rather than resistance.

True wealth isn't just about what you have. It's about how you live.

The greatest financial mistake isn't poor investing or overspending—it's believing that wealth is something you achieve rather than something you embody. It's postponing joy for some future number. It's separating your money life from your real life.

But what if wealth could feel as natural as breathing? What if your financial practices could align perfectly with who you are?

Integrating Wealth

The journey from 'doing' wealth to being wealthy begins with a fundamental shift in perspective. When we treat wealth as something to achieve rather than embody, we create an artificial separation between our financial lives and our authentic selves. This disconnect often manifests as constant striving, perpetual postponement of joy, and a sense that wealth remains forever just out of reach. True integration happens when we recognize wealth not as a destination but as a way of moving through the world.

This integration requires us to bridge the gap between our financial goals and daily lifestyle choices. Rather than viewing our present circumstances as merely stepping stones to future abundance, we can begin weaving wealth consciousness into every aspect of our lives. This might mean bringing mindfulness to our spending decisions, approaching our career with a spirit of abundance, or simply allowing ourselves to experience prosperity in small, meaningful ways each day.

Creating sustainable success through integration demands that we align our money practices with our deeper values and natural rhythms. When our financial choices flow from our authentic selves rather than external pressures or arbitrary benchmarks, we discover a form of wealth that feels effortless and regenerative. This doesn't mean abandoning ambitious goals or practical planning. Rather, it means ensuring these elements arise organically from our true nature instead of being imposed from outside.

The process of integration also involves examining where we might be creating unnecessary friction in our relationship with wealth. Often, we maintain unconscious barriers between ourselves and abundance, treating money as something foreign to, or separate from, our essential nature. By recognizing these self-imposed boundaries, we can begin dissolving them, allowing wealth to flow more naturally through every aspect of our lives.

The ultimate aim of wealth integration is to create seamless harmony between our financial practices and our authentic selves. When we achieve this alignment, making money decisions becomes as natural as breathing, and our relationship with wealth transforms from one of struggle to one of flow. This integrated approach allows us to experience abundance not as a future state to be achieved but as our natural way of being in the present moment.

The Harmony Principle

True wealth emerges from the delicate balance between ambition and contentment. This isn't just philosophical wisdom. A 2023 Deloitte well-being study found that individuals who align their financial decisions with their values report 47% higher satisfaction with their financial lives. When we integrate our money choices with our deeper truth, we don't just build wealth—we create fulfillment.

While society often presents these as opposing forces, they actually function as complementary energies that, when properly aligned, create a powerful foundation for sustainable abundance. This balance allows us to pursue meaningful goals while remaining deeply present in the richness available at each moment.

At its core, this principle challenges the prevalent either/or mentality that plagues many people's relationship with wealth. We don't have to choose between building financial success and maintaining well-being, growing our resources and enjoying what we have, or planning for tomorrow and living fully today. Instead, we can cultivate a both/and approach that honors all aspects of our wealth journey.

The art of integrating wealth with well-being requires us to expand our definition of prosperity beyond mere financial metrics. We discover a more holistic form of abundance when we measure our success by the quality of our relationships, the depth of our satisfaction, and the alignment with our values. This broader perspective allows us to make decisions that serve both our financial growth and overall flourishing.

Creating sustainable growth through harmony means paying attention to our life's natural rhythms of expansion and consolidation. Just as nature moves through seasons, our wealth journey includes periods of intense growth and periods of integration. By honoring these cycles, rather than fighting against them, we create a more sustainable path to prosperity that doesn't sacrifice our well-being for financial gain.

Perhaps most importantly, the harmony principle invites us to live our values now rather than wait for some future wealth threshold. This means finding ways to express our deepest principles through our current financial choices, whether building a business, investing our resources, or making daily spending decisions. When we align our present actions with our core values, we create a sense of congruence that naturally attracts greater abundance.

Living in harmony with wealth also means recognizing that our financial journey is not separate from our spiritual, emotional, and physical well-being. As we learn to balance these different aspects of our lives, we discover that each area enriches the others. Our financial decisions become more intuitive when guided by inner wisdom, while our spiritual practice is grounded in practical action. This integration creates a virtuous cycle where each aspect of our life supports and enhances the others.

Transformational Moment: The Integration Inventory

Take a moment to find a quiet space where you can reflect deeply. With gentle awareness, we'll explore your relationship with wealth across different areas of your life. Rather than judging what you discover, simply observe with curiosity where money flows naturally and where it feels like you're pushing against resistance.

Begin by considering your daily financial interactions—paying bills, making purchases, or checking accounts. Notice which of these activities feel light and easy and which create tension in your body. What emotions arise when you engage with money in these everyday moments? Where do you find yourself holding your breath or rushing through the experience?

Now expand your awareness to your more significant financial decisions— investing, career choices, major purchases. When do these choices feel aligned with your authentic self? Where do they seem to come from, external pressure or "should" statements? Notice the quality of energy around each type of decision. Does wealth feel like a natural extension of who you are in these moments, or does it feel like a role you're trying to play?

Let your attention move to your relationships and how money flows through them. Where do financial discussions and decisions feel comfortable and transparent? Where do you sense constriction or avoidance? Notice any patterns in how you show up differently around money with different people in your life.

Consider your aspirations and long-term vision. Which of your financial goals emerge from a genuine sense of purpose and excitement? Which ones carry a weight of obligation or fear? Notice where your future dreams feel expansive and inspiring versus where they feel heavy with pressure to achieve or prove something.

Now, explore your current lifestyle choices. Where do you naturally express abundance without thinking about it? Where do you find yourself restricting or controlling out of scarcity? Notice the areas of your life where wealth flows freely and where it feels blocked or constrained.

Finally, take a moment to reflect on your money practices and habits. Which ones feel like they were consciously chosen to align with your values? Which ones seem inherited or adopted without question? Notice where your financial routines support your well-being and where they might be creating unnecessary struggle.

Let all these observations settle into your awareness without trying to change anything. Simply acknowledging where wealth feels natural and where it feels forced is the first step toward greater integration. In the coming sections, we'll explore how to transform these insights into aligned action, but for now, allow yourself to sit with what you've discovered.

Consider capturing your reflections in writing, noting specific examples in each area where you found either flow or friction. These personal insights will serve as valuable guideposts as you continue your journey toward embodied wealth.

Remember, the goal isn't to judge or immediately fix what you've observed but to bring conscious awareness to your current relationship with wealth. This awareness itself begins the process of natural transformation toward greater integration.

Integration Barriers

The path to integrated wealth often encounters predictable yet profound barriers that can subtly hold us back from experiencing true abundance. Understanding and gently dissolving these barriers becomes essential for creating lasting transformation in our relationship with wealth.

The most pervasive barrier often appears as "I'll be happy when..." thinking. This mindset creates an artificial divide between our present reality and future fulfillment, perpetually pushing joy and satisfaction just beyond our reach. Whether the condition is a specific number in our bank account, a career milestone, or a financial achievement; this pattern keeps us locked in a state of perpetual waiting, preventing us from experiencing the abundance already present in our lives.

Closely related is the barrier of "I can't enjoy it yet," a form of self-imposed restriction that stems from believing we haven't earned the right to experience pleasure or abundance in the present moment. This barrier often manifests as an inability to appreciate our current resources fully, celebrate our progress, or allow ourselves simple pleasures without guilt. It creates a pattern of continuous deferral that can persist even as our wealth grows.

The trap of either/or thinking represents another significant barrier. It leads us to believe we must choose between financial success and personal fulfillment, between saving for the future and enjoying the present, or between practical decisions and passionate pursuits. This false dichotomy keeps us locked in unnecessary struggles, preventing us from seeing the creative possibilities that emerge when we embrace both seemingly opposing aspects of our wealth journey.

Perhaps the most subtle yet powerful barrier is the sensation that "wealth feels foreign"—a deep-seated belief that abundance is somehow not natural to who we are. This can manifest as imposter syndrome when success arrives, discomfort with charging for the value we provide, or difficulty receiving money and opportunities. This barrier often originates in our early experiences and cultural conditioning around money, requiring gentle but persistent work to transform.

These barriers share a common thread: They all stem from learned patterns rather than inherent truths about wealth. The good news is that what has been learned can be unlearned, replaced with more empowering perspectives that allow wealth to flow naturally. The key lies not in forcing these barriers down through sheer will but in understanding them with compassion and gradually creating new patterns that align with our authentic relationship to abundance.

Transforming these barriers requires consistent awareness and gentle persistence. As we notice these patterns arising in our daily lives, we can choose to pause, question their validity, and consciously create new responses that support, rather than restrict, our wealth integration. This process of barrier dissolution happens not through struggle but through increasing awareness and conscious choice.

Creating Your Wealth Lifestyle

Creating your wealth lifestyle begins with identifying you core values—the fundamental principles guiding your authentic expression in the world. This process goes beyond simply listing admirable qualities to deeply examining what truly matters to you when all external pressures are stripped away. Your core values serve as the compass for all financial decisions, from daily spending choices to long-term investment strategies. They might include freedom, creativity, security, contribution, or growth, but what matters most is that they genuinely resonate with your deepest truth rather than reflecting what others think you should value.

Aligning money with purpose transforms wealth from a mere accumulation of resources into a powerful vehicle for meaningful impact. This alignment requires exploring how your financial choices can actively support your life's mission and deepest aspirations. It involves asking questions like how your work contributes to something larger than yourself, how your investments reflect your vision for the world, and how your spending supports what you want to create. When money becomes a tool for expressing purpose, the entire experience of wealth shifts from obligation to inspiration.

Incorporating practices that create joy introduces an element often missing from traditional financial planning—the conscious cultivation of pleasure and satisfaction in our relationship with wealth. These practices might include regular celebrations of financial milestones, mindful spending rituals that heighten our appreciation of resources, or simple daily acknowledgments of abundance. The key is making joy a deliberate practice rather than an accidental occurrence, weaving moments of delight into the fabric of our financial life rather than postponing them for some future achievement.

Building sustainable systems ensures your wealth lifestyle can flourish over time without constant effort or willpower. These systems include practical financial infrastructure—automated savings, investment strategies, and money management tools—and personal practices supporting your well-being. The goal is to create structures that make wealth flow naturally while honoring your energy and natural rhythms. This might mean setting up regular financial review rituals, establishing clear boundaries around money decisions, or creating support networks that encourage sustainable wealth practices.

Living wealth now represents the ultimate integration of all these elements into the present-moment experience. This means moving beyond the idea of wealth as a future state to embodying your relationship with abundance in every moment. It involves bringing conscious awareness to how you carry yourself, make decisions, and interact with money daily. Rather than waiting to feel wealthy when certain conditions are met, you begin expressing wealth consciousness through your current choices and actions, regardless of external circumstances.

This framework creates a holistic approach where each element supports and enhances the others. Your core values inform your purpose, which shapes your joy practices, which in turn require sustainable systems to maintain.

All of this comes together in your present-moment experience of wealth. The result is a naturally integrated wealth lifestyle that feels both authentic and sustainable, allowing abundance to flow through all aspects of your life with greater ease and alignment.

The power of this framework lies not just in its individual components but in how they work together to create a cohesive whole. When all five elements are in harmony, wealth becomes less about following external rules or reaching arbitrary targets and more about expressing your unique path to abundance. This integration allows you to create a wealth lifestyle, supporting your financial goals and enriching your life experience.

Creating Sustainable Success

Creating sustainable success in your wealth journey requires a fundamentally different approach from the typical push-and-hustle mentality that often leads to burnout. The key lies in developing wealth routines that feel as natural as breathing, allowing abundance to flow through your life without constant strain or effort. These routines should emerge from your authentic rhythms rather than being forced upon you by external expectations or artificial deadlines.

Building lasting habits around wealth requires understanding that small, consistent actions create more sustainable change than dramatic gestures. This might mean establishing a daily five-minute financial check-in that feels genuinely doable rather than committing to hour-long planning sessions that become overwhelming. The focus shifts from perfection to progression, allowing these habits to take root naturally in the soil of your daily life.

Designing joy practices becomes essential for maintaining long-term momentum in your wealth journey. These practices serve as regular reminders to celebrate progress, acknowledge abundance, and find pleasure in your relationship with money. Rather than treating financial management as a burden to be endured, joy practices transform it into an opportunity for connection with your deeper purpose and values.

Maintaining balance in your wealth journey involves recognizing that sustainability isn't about rigid consistency but rather dynamic equilibrium. Just as a tightrope walker makes constant micro-adjustments to stay upright, maintaining financial well-being requires ongoing attention to the shifting demands of life. This means developing the flexibility to adapt your practices while keeping your core values steady.

Success becomes truly sustainable when we learn to navigate the natural cycles of expansion and consolidation in our financial lives. There will be periods of intense growth and activity balanced by times of reflection and integration. Understanding and honoring these rhythms prevents the exhaustion of maintaining constant forward momentum.

Creating systems that support your wealth journey while honoring your energy levels and natural tendencies allows for more effortless progress over time. This might involve automating specific financial tasks, establishing clear decision-making frameworks, or creating support networks that help maintain momentum during challenging periods. The goal is to reduce the cognitive and emotional load of managing wealth while maximizing its positive impact on your life.

True sustainability in wealth creation comes from aligning your financial practices with your broader life aspirations. When your approach to money supports rather than detracts from your overall well-being, you create a foundation for lasting success that doesn't require sacrificing what matters most to you. This integration allows wealth to become a natural expression of who you are rather than a separate pursuit that demands constant attention and effort.

Wealth Wisdom Reflection

1. Where does wealth feel forced?

2. What would natural wealth look like?

3. How can you bring more joy now?

4. What needs to be integrated?

From Scarcity To Sovereignty

When Nicky first started coaching with me, she carried herself with the careful restraint of someone who had learned early to take up as little space as possible. As one of ten children raised by a single parent, she had grown up intimately acquainted with scarcity. The memory of walking to school with holes in her shoes wasn't just a distant childhood experience—it had become the lens through which she viewed her entire relationship with money.

"I remember sitting in our first session," Nicky told me recently, "and you asked me to envision my ideal wealthy life. I couldn't do it. It was like trying to imagine a color I'd never seen before. Whenever I tried to picture myself with abundance, my childhood experiences would rush in and shut down the possibility."

The transformation began when we started exploring how her early experiences still made her financial decisions in the present. Every time she set her prices, her past whispered that she should be grateful for whatever she could get. When opportunities for growth appeared, the memory of lack would convince her to play it safe.

"The breakthrough came when I realized I was still living in my childhood story," Nicky reflected. "I was running a successful business, but I was pricing my services based on what my younger self thought she deserved, not what my expertise was actually worth."

Working together, we began the delicate process of separating past survival patterns from present possibilities. Rather than trying to override her early experiences, we acknowledged how they had helped her survive while gently creating space for a new story to emerge.

Today, Nicky's transformation is evident in her increased pricing, growing business success, and how she carries herself. She no longer apologizes for taking up space or creating wealth. Her childhood experiences haven't disappeared—they've been integrated into her story of resilience rather than remaining a barrier to her abundance.

"I used to think wealth wasn't for people like me," she says now, a quiet confidence in her voice. "But I've learned that my background doesn't disqualify me from abundance—if anything, it's given me a deeper appreciation for what it means to create wealth on my terms."

Nicky's journey from scarcity to conscious wealth creation is a powerful reminder that our past circumstances don't have to define our future relationship with abundance. Through conscious integration, even our deepest wounds can be transformed into wisdom, allowing us to create wealth that honors where we've come from and where we choose to go.

Mastering Integration

The journey of mastering integration brings us to the subtle, yet crucial, aspects of maintaining wealth consciousness through life's inevitable changes. Handling growth phases becomes an art of expanding your financial capacity and your ability to receive and manage increased abundance with grace. This means developing the emotional and practical infrastructure to support each new level of wealth while maintaining your core values and sense of self.

Navigating transitions—whether financial windfalls, market downturns, or life changes—requires deep trust in your integrated wealth foundation. Rather than being thrown off course by external circumstances, you learn to move through changes with flexibility while staying anchored in your wealth consciousness. This resilience comes not from rigid control but from the confidence that your relationship with abundance transcends temporary conditions.

Building resilience in your wealth journey involves creating multiple layers of support—practical, emotional, and spiritual. This might include maintaining living expenses funds (i.e., emergency funds) while cultivating supportive relationships and regular practices that ground you in abundance regardless of external circumstances. True resilience emerges from knowing that your wealth identity isn't dependent on specific numbers but on your internal relationship with abundance.

Celebrating life becomes an occasional event and a fundamental practice in mastering integration. This means acknowledging both the major milestones and the small daily moments of abundance that make up your wealth journey. Regular celebration helps embed the experience of sufficiency and success into your nervous system, making it easier to maintain positive momentum through challenges.

Your wealth isn't separate from your life; it's an expression of who you are. As you integrate these practices, you'll find yourself living with more ease, creating natural abundance, and experiencing joy along the journey. The artificial boundaries between your financial life and your authentic self dissolve, revealing a more harmonious way of being with wealth.

Each step you take toward integration—whether it's establishing a new morning ritual, refining your wealth boundaries, or celebrating a moment of abundance—builds upon the others, creating a solid foundation for sustainable prosperity. This isn't about reaching a final destination but about continuously evolving your relationship with wealth in ways that feel true to who you are.

In our final chapter, we'll explore how to expand this integration into a lasting legacy, but first, take a moment to reflect. How is wealth asking to be lived through you? What aspects of your financial life are ready to be more fully integrated with your authentic self? What would it feel like to allow abundance to flow as naturally as breathing through every aspect of your being?

Remember that true mastery isn't about perfect control but about perfect trust—trust in your ability to navigate the journey, the practices you've developed, and the wisdom that emerges when you allow wealth to be a natural expression of your highest self. As you continue to embrace this integrated approach to wealth, you'll discover that abundance becomes not something you chase but something you naturally embody.

KEY TAKEAWAYS:

- True wealth is a way of being, not just having
- Integration creates sustainable abundance
- Harmony between wealth and wellbeing is essential
- Living wealth now transforms future results

CHAPTER 9

Living Your Legacy

The warm afternoon sun streams through my office window as I review my latest financial statement, tears welling in my eyes. But these aren't tears of stress or worry; they're tears of profound gratitude and realization. Just this morning, I set up an account that would allow my mother to retire from the domestic work she's done tirelessly since I was a newborn. For over four decades, she cleaned other people's homes, cared for other families' children and aging parents, and even did landscaping and construction-type projects, all while dreaming of a better future for her own children.

I close my eyes and remember the countless mornings I'd wake to find her already gone, her love expressed in the breakfast she made us right before walking out the door. Despite working long hours, she somehow found the energy to instill in my brothers and me the importance of giving to those with less than us. Even in those lean years, when dinner was sometimes more creativity than substance, she'd still find ways to help others in our community. "We may not have much," she'd say, sorting through our modest groceries and slightly used clothes we'd outgrown to share with a struggling neighbor, "but we have enough to share."

Now, as I ensure she never has to clean another house or worry about her next paycheck, I feel the weight of this moment. This isn't just a financial transaction—it's the fulfillment of a dream that started before I could walk.

My mother's sacrifices, her unwavering belief in possibility, and her insistence on generosity, even in scarcity, have laid the foundation for this transformation.

The significance of this moment extends far beyond my mother's retirement. As my coach Lisa Nichols always reminds me, "When good people do well, good people simply do more good in the world." I think about my future children, who will grow up knowing abundance not as a distant dream but as their starting point. They won't have to wonder if there's enough—they'll be able to focus on how to enjoy and share what they have.

Yet even as I celebrate this milestone, I recognize that true wealth isn't just about accumulating resources—it's about amplifying impact. The financial transformation I've undergone isn't merely personal; it's a pivot point in my family's story. It's the moment when generations of financial struggle transform into a legacy of abundance and giving.

Looking at the retirement account I set up for my mother, I see more than numbers. I know the end of one chapter and the beginning of another. I know the power of transformation to heal our present circumstances and future possibilities. Most importantly, I see the truth that financial empowerment isn't just about personal gain; it's about positioning ourselves to create positive change in the lives of others.

This journey of financial transformation has shown me that when we heal our relationship with money, we don't just change our lives. We create new possibilities for everyone our lives touch. We break generational patterns of sacrifice and struggle. We establish new templates of abundance and generosity that will echo through time.

Legacy isn't what you leave behind. It's what you live forward.

Each time you honor your worth, speak your truth, or make an empowered choice, you're not just changing your life. You're creating new possibilities for generations to come. You're healing money stories that have been passed down for decades. You're writing a new chapter in your family's financial story.

The question isn't whether you'll leave a legacy. The question is: What legacy are you creating right now?

Beyond the Bank Account

Understanding true legacy begins with recognizing that wealth extends far beyond monetary assets. While financial inheritance plays its role, your true legacy lies in the invisible ripples of transformation you create through your relationship with money. This deeper understanding of legacy encompasses the values you embody, the wisdom you share, and the patterns you choose to break or perpetuate. When you grasp that legacy is lived rather than left, every financial decision becomes an opportunity to align your actions with your highest values and create a lasting impact.

The ripple effect of transformation starts small but expands exponentially. Like a stone dropped in still water, each conscious choice about money sends waves outward, touching lives in ways you might never see. When you choose to heal your relationship with money, that healing reverberates through your family system. When you set healthy financial boundaries, you demonstrate to others what's possible. Your personal growth becomes a catalyst for collective transformation, inspiring others to examine their relationship with wealth and possibility.

Breaking generational patterns requires both courage and compassion. These patterns—whether of overspending, hoarding, financial avoidance, or scarcity thinking—have often been passed down through generations, each person unconsciously carrying forward the money wounds of their ancestors. You gain the power to interrupt these patterns by bringing awareness to them. This isn't about judgment or blame; it's about conscious choice. Each time you pause before making a financial decision and choose differently than your conditioning would dictate, you create a break in the pattern that benefits you and all who come after you.

The Federal Reserve's 2023 Survey of Consumer Finances confirms that children whose parents discuss financial decisions with them are 65% more likely to save regularly. Moreover, Charles Schwab's 2023 study found that 65% of Americans say their parents' financial habits significantly influenced their own relationship with money.

Creating new money stories is perhaps the most powerful aspect of legacy work. These stories aren't just about numbers in a bank account; they're about worth, possibility, and abundance. When you begin to author new narratives about your relationship with money, you permit others to do the same. Your story of transformation from scarcity to abundance, from fear to confidence, from shame to empowerment becomes a blueprint for others. Every time you share your journey, whether through words or actions, you're contributing to a larger narrative of what's possible in a relationship with money.

The impact of your financial transformation extends far beyond your personal balance sheet. It influences how your children view their worth, how your friends approach their financial decisions, and how your community thinks about abundance. This broader perspective of legacy invites you to consider what you'll leave behind and what you're living forward every day. It challenges you to see every financial choice as an opportunity to demonstrate what's possible when you align your money with your values and vision for the future.

The Legacy You're Living

Your relationship with money creates immediate and lasting impact on those around you, often in ways you might not even realize. Your children notice when you shift your money mindset from scarcity to abundance. When you advocate for your worth at work, your colleagues are watching. Your friends observe when you make conscious spending choices aligned with your values. These changes ripple outward, subtly influencing how others perceive their relationship with money. Each time you choose courage over comfort in your financial decisions, you demonstrate what's possible for others who witness your journey.

Transforming family money dynamics begins with your own shift in consciousness and behavior. As you heal your relationship with money, old family patterns naturally start to evolve. The aunt who always commented on everyone's spending habits may find herself reflecting on her own money stories. The sibling who avoided financial discussions might start asking questions about investing. Your changed behavior creates a safe space for others to explore their own relationship with wealth. This transformation doesn't require confrontation or forced conversations; it happens organically as you model a healthier approach to money.

Creating community wealth extends beyond individual prosperity. As your financial confidence grows, you become better equipped to contribute to collective abundance. This might manifest as mentoring others in your professional field, sharing resources within your community, or collaborating on projects that generate shared wealth. Understanding that abundance multiplies through sharing naturally makes you a catalyst for community prosperity. Your financial empowerment becomes a resource that strengthens the economic fabric of your entire community.

Building generational wisdom involves consciously passing down assets, financial intelligence, and emotional well-being around money. This wisdom transmission happens through both words and actions. When your children see you making mindful spending decisions, they absorb lessons about value and choice. When your nieces and nephews witness you discussing money openly and without shame, they learn that financial conversations can be healthy and empowering. Each interaction becomes an opportunity to demonstrate what a balanced, conscious relationship with money looks like.

The legacy you're living isn't about perfection but progression and authenticity. Some days, you'll navigate financial decisions with grace and confidence; other days, you'll stumble and learn. Both experiences contribute to the legacy you're creating. Being transparent about your journey, including the challenges and victories, shows others that financial empowerment is an evolving process. Your willingness to be visible in your struggles and successes allows others to embrace their financial growth journey.

This living legacy manifests in daily choices and interactions: how you talk about money with your partner, the financial boundaries you set with family, the generosity you extend to others, and the way you honor your worth. Each of these moments shapes not just your financial future but influences the money stories of everyone in your orbit. Your lived example becomes a powerful force for transformation, creating new possibilities for how future generations relate to wealth and abundance.

Transformational Moment: The Legacy Vision

Close your eyes and take a deep breath. Allow yourself to settle into this moment of reflection and possibility. We're going to take a journey into the impact of your financial transformation, not just on your own life, but on the lives that your journey touches and transforms.

Imagine standing in a room surrounded by mirrors stretching from floor to ceiling. Each mirror represents a different aspect of your legacy—the changes you're creating, the wisdom you're sharing, and the patterns you're breaking. As you look into the first mirror, see yourself as you are now, standing in your growing financial power. Notice how differently you carry yourself compared to just months ago. Observe the confidence in your stance, the clarity in your eyes, and the peace in your expression.

Now, turn to the next mirror. In this reflection, see the people closest to you—your family, dear friends, and immediate community. Watch how your transformation ripples through their lives. Perhaps you see your children approaching money with confidence instead of fear. Maybe you glimpse friends having more open conversations about wealth because of your example. Notice how your changed relationship with money creates new possibilities in all your relationships.

In the third mirror, look deeper into time. See the generations that will come after you. Witness how your courage to transform your money story creates a new legacy of possibility. Watch as the money wounds passed down through your family line begin to heal. Observe how your conscious choices today create new patterns of prosperity and peace for those who will follow in your footsteps.

The fourth mirror shows your broader impact—the lives you may never directly engage with but are touched by your transformation. See how your example creates ripples of change in your community. Notice how your financial empowerment enables you to contribute in bigger ways. Witness how your story inspires others to begin their journey of financial healing.

Now, in the final mirror, see yourself five years from now. This version of you has lived these new patterns consistently. Notice how naturally you embody your worth. Observe the ease with which you navigate money decisions. Feel the deep satisfaction of knowing your transformation has created lasting change, not just for you but also for countless others.

Take a moment to write down what you saw in each mirror:

- What changes did you notice in yourself?
- What impact did you witness in your immediate circle?
- What patterns did you see shifting for future generations?
- How did your transformation affect your broader community?
- What possibilities opened up in your five-year vision?

Let this vision serve as both anchor and compass. Return to it when you need a reminder of the bigger purpose of your financial journey. Your transformation isn't just about you—it's about every life your example touches, every pattern you help break, and every possibility you help create.

Remember, the legacy you're building isn't some distant future event. It's being created in every choice you make today. Each time you honor your worth, speak your truth about money or make an empowered financial decision, you're living your legacy forward. You're showing others what's possible. You're creating new pathways of prosperity that will benefit generations to come.

Take one more deep breath and open your eyes. Carry this expanded vision of your impact with you. Let it inform your choices and inspire your actions.

Your financial transformation is a gift that keeps giving, touching lives in ways you may never fully know.

Legacy Barriers

As you create a new financial legacy, you'll likely encounter internal resistance and external challenges. Understanding these common barriers—and their breakthrough solutions—can help you navigate this territory with greater ease and confidence.

"Who am I to create change?" This whisper of self-doubt often emerges just as you begin to see the possibility of your impact. It stems from old stories about your worth and right to influence others. The breakthrough comes in recognizing that your journey itself qualifies you. You don't need special credentials or perfect finances to create positive change. Every time you've faced a money challenge and chosen differently, every time you've learned from a financial mistake, every step you've taken toward healing your relationship with wealth—these experiences are exactly what makes you qualified. Your honest journey, including its struggles and victories, makes your example powerful and relatable to others.

"My family won't understand" speaks to the fear of disrupting established patterns and expectations. Perhaps you come from a long line of people who viewed money through a lens of scarcity, or maybe financial discussions were strictly taboo in your household. The breakthrough here lies in understanding that you don't need everyone's understanding to create change. Your role isn't to convince or convert others—it's to live your truth consistently. When you maintain healthy financial boundaries and model new behaviors with compassion, understanding often follows naturally. Remember, resistance from family often means you're successfully disrupting patterns that need to change.

"It's too late to start" reflects a common myth that legacy work has an expiration date. Whether in your thirties or your seventies, this barrier can make you question if your changes can truly make a difference. The breakthrough comes in realizing that legacy creation is about the present moment, not some distant future. Every age and stage of life offers unique opportunities for impact. Sometimes, starting later means you bring more wisdom and life experience to your transformation. Your journey might actually be more powerful because of, not despite, its timing.

"I'm just one person" underestimates the exponential nature of personal transformation. This barrier shows up as doubt about whether individual changes can really affect larger systems and patterns. The breakthrough emerges when you understand the ripple effect of personal change. Every major movement and transformation started with one person choosing differently. Your individual choice to heal your relationship with money, model financial empowerment, and speak openly about wealth creates waves of possibility that extend far beyond your immediate circle. You may never know all the lives you touch through your example.

Each of these barriers represents a growth edge—an opportunity to deepen your commitment to creating lasting change. When you encounter them, treat them as signposts rather than stopping points. They often indicate that you're pushing beyond comfortable territory into real transformation. The key is not to avoid these barriers but to use them as springboards for deeper understanding and more intentional action.

Remember that breakthroughs don't always look like dramatic change. Sometimes, it's as subtle as choosing to have an honest conversation about money when you'd rather avoid it. Other times, it's setting a boundary that honors your financial well-being, even when others push back. Each small act of courage accumulates, creating a foundation for a larger transformation.

Your legacy work doesn't require perfection; it requires presence and persistence. When these barriers arise, return to your deeper purpose. Remember that every person who created positive change faced doubt, resistance, and uncertainty. What set them apart was their willingness to continue despite these challenges, holding faith in the possibility of transformation.

Crafting Your Legacy

Creating a meaningful financial legacy requires intentional action and conscious awareness. This framework provides a structured approach to building lasting impact through five essential steps that build upon each other to create transformative change.

1. Healing the Past

The foundation of your legacy work begins with healing your inherited money stories. This involves acknowledging the financial patterns, beliefs, and behaviors you've carried from your family system. Start by examining your earliest money memories. What did you learn about wealth from your parents and grandparents? What financial traumas or triumphs shaped your relationship with money? This isn't about blame or judgment; it's about understanding the roots of your money story so you can consciously choose which patterns to carry forward and which to transform.

Take time to honor the resilience and wisdom in your lineage, even amid struggle. Perhaps your grandmother's frugality during hard times taught valuable lessons about resourcefulness. Maybe your father's financial mistakes offer important insights about risk and trust. As you heal these stories, you free yourself—and future generations—from unconscious patterns that no longer serve.

2. Transforming the Present

With awareness of your past patterns, you can begin actively reshaping your current relationship with money. This transformation happens through daily choices and conscious actions. Each time you check your bank account without anxiety, discuss money openly with loved ones or make financial decisions aligned with your values, you're creating new neural pathways and behavioral patterns.

Focus on embodying the financial qualities you want to pass on. If you want future generations to approach money with confidence, practice making confident money decisions now. If you want your legacy to include generosity, look for opportunities to share resources wisely. Your present actions become the template for others to follow.

3. Creating the Future

Legacy building requires vision—a clear sense of the possibilities you want to create for future generations. This goes beyond financial goals to encompass the values, wisdom, and opportunities you want to generate. Consider questions like: What financial freedoms do you want your children to inherit? What money wisdom do you want your community to gain from your example? How can your wealth create a positive impact long after you're gone?

Write your vision in detail, allowing yourself to dream beyond current limitations. Include both tangible outcomes (like educational funds or sustainable businesses) and intangible impacts (like financial confidence or abundant mindset). This vision becomes your north star, guiding your decisions and actions.

4. Expanding Your Influence

As your personal transformation deepens, look for ways to consciously expand your impact. This might begin with simple conversations about money lessons learned, then grow into mentoring others in financial literacy or creating resources for your community. Consider how your experience and insights could benefit others on their money-healing journey.

Remember that influence expands naturally when it comes from authentic transformation. You don't need to force or push your message—simply share your truth and allow others to take what resonates. Your vulnerability in discussing both successes and struggles can create powerful connections and inspiration.

5. Living Your Message

The most powerful legacy comes from consistent alignment between your words and actions. This means walking your talk in both small and large ways. When you say you value financial independence, your choices should reflect this. When you speak about the importance of generous giving, your actions should demonstrate this value.

Living your message also means staying committed to your own growth. Continue educating yourself about wealth building, remain open to new perspectives on money, and be willing to adjust your approach as you learn and evolve. Your dedication to ongoing learning becomes part of the legacy you create.

Integration Tools

To support this framework, implement daily practices that reinforce your legacy work:

The Legacy Light Practice: Begin each day by connecting with your larger purpose. Take a few moments to visualize the positive impact your financial choices are creating. Feel the connection between your present actions and the future possibilities they're generating.

Your Legacy Blueprint: Create a detailed map of your desired impact across different areas:

- Personal transformation goals
- Family wealth education plans
- Community contribution intentions
- Knowledge and wisdom-sharing strategies

Review and update this blueprint quarterly, celebrating progress and adjusting actions as needed.

Remember that crafting your legacy is not a linear process—it's a dynamic journey of continuous growth and expansion. Some days, you'll feel the power of your impact clearly; other days, you may require recommitment to your vision. Trust that each step forward, no matter how small, contributes to the larger transformation you're creating.

Teaching Through Example

The most powerful form of financial education doesn't come from lectures or lessons—it emerges naturally through lived examples. When you embody healthy money relationships and conscious wealth practices, you create informal teaching moments that impact others more deeply than any formal instruction ever could. Your daily actions and attitudes toward money speak volumes, creating ripples of influence that extend far beyond your immediate circle. This silent teaching happens continuously, whether you're aware of it or not, making it essential to bring consciousness to how you model financial well-being.

Modeling Healthy Money Relationships

Your relationship with money tells a story that others read clearly, even when no words are spoken. Each time you check your bank balance with calm curiosity instead of anxiety, you demonstrate a new possibility. When you make purchasing decisions from a place of value alignment rather than emotional impulse, you show others what conscious consumption looks like in practice. These seemingly small moments create powerful learning opportunities for those around you, especially those who may be struggling with their own money relationship. By handling physical money with respect, discussing financial decisions with thoughtful consideration, and expressing gratitude for both small and large financial blessings, you create a template for others to follow. Your ability to address money challenges with problem-solving energy instead of shame and to celebrate financial wins without apology or minimization shows others what's possible in their own journey with wealth.

Sharing Wisdom with Grace

The transmission of financial wisdom happens most effectively through natural conversation and authentic sharing rather than formal teaching or preaching. When you position yourself as a fellow traveler on the money journey rather than an expert, you create openings for genuine connection and learning. These moments often arise organically when someone expresses frustration with their finances or seeks guidance on a money decision. By sharing your own experiences with vulnerability and honesty, you create safe spaces for others to explore their own relationship with money. Your willingness to discuss both successes and struggles helps normalize conversations about wealth and breaks down the taboos that often surround financial discussions. The key lies in offering your insights as possibilities rather than prescriptions, always acknowledging that different approaches work for different people, and respecting each person's unique financial journey.

Creating Teaching Moments

While teaching happens naturally through example, bringing awareness to organic teaching opportunities can amplify your positive impact. These moments present themselves frequently—when someone asks your opinion about a financial decision, when you're making a conscious money choice in front of others, or when financial topics arise in casual conversation. Rather than launching into advice-giving mode, these moments invite you to share your journey and insights in ways that empower others to find their own path. By paying attention to these opportunities and responding with authenticity and compassion, you create informal learning experiences that often prove more impactful than any planned lesson could be. The key lies in recognizing these moments as opportunities for connection and growth rather than platforms for showcasing your financial wisdom.

Building Confidence in Others

Perhaps the most profound aspect of teaching through example is its ability to help others discover their own financial capabilities. As you model confidence in money matters, you create a permission field for others to step into their power. This happens through consistent encouragement without pressure, celebrating others' money wins no matter how small, and expressing genuine confidence in their ability to learn and grow. Rather than providing answers, you can ask questions that help others uncover their own wisdom: "What feels right to you in this situation?" or "What would your most confident self do?" Combined with your living example of financial empowerment, these questions create a supportive environment for others to explore and expand their relationship with money.

The power of teaching through example lies not in perfection but in authenticity. Your financial journey, including its challenges and missteps, becomes a roadmap others can follow. When you handle mistakes with grace and approach setbacks as learning opportunities, you demonstrate resilience and growth mindset in action. This real-world modeling of financial wellness, complete with its ups and downs, offers others a realistic template for their own transformation. Consistent alignment between your words and actions creates a legacy of financial wisdom that spreads naturally through your community and beyond.

Remember that teaching through example requires consistency between your words and actions. If you speak about the importance of saving but consistently overspend, your actions will teach more powerfully than your words. This doesn't mean you need to be perfect—in fact, handling financial mistakes with grace and learning is itself a powerful teaching opportunity.

Your role as a financial exemplar isn't about having all the answers or never making mistakes. It's about demonstrating what's possible when you approach money with consciousness, commitment, and compassion. Each time you make an empowered money choice, handle a financial challenge with grace, or share your journey with authenticity, you create a template others can follow.

Wealth Wisdom Reflection:

1. What patterns are you breaking?

2. Who is watching your journey?

3. What wisdom are you discovering?

4. What possibility are you creating?

Breaking Ground, Breaking Patterns: A Legacy of Possibility

My phone pinged one sunny Tuesday afternoon. When I glanced at the screen, the message brought tears to my eyes: "I could have never done this without you. Thank you so much." Attached was a photo of Robin, beaming with pride, standing in front of a sleek modern house—her house—built from the ground up to her exact specifications.

The image took me back to our first meeting three years earlier. Robin sat across from me, shoulders hunched, barely able to look at her bank statements. Money conversations made her physically uncomfortable. Years of financial struggle and inherited beliefs about what was possible for "people like us" had left deep wounds. Her family's story was one of perpetual renting, of always living on someone else's property, of never quite believing home ownership was within reach.

"My grandmother rented. My mother rents. That's just what we do," she had told me then, her voice carrying the weight of generational resignation. But beneath that weight, I heard something else—a tiny spark of hope, a whisper of "what if?"

That spark was all we needed. Together, we began the careful work of transformation. It wasn't just about fixing her credit score or creating a spending plan, though we did both with methodical precision. It wasn't just about crafting a debt repayment strategy that would finally break the chains of financial burden. The real work, the deep work, was in excavating those buried beliefs about money and worth that had been passed down through generations like unwanted heirlooms.

Week by week, month by month, we replaced limiting beliefs with expansive ones. "I'll always be a renter" became "I'm building generational wealth." "That's not for people like me" transformed into "I define what's possible for me." Each small victory built momentum: her first savings milestone, her debt-free celebration, the day her credit score crossed 800.

As I looked at the photo of Robin standing proudly in front of her custom-built home, I saw more than just a successful client. I saw a woman who had broken a generational pattern. I saw the end of a legacy of limitation and the beginning of a legacy of possibility. Robin wasn't just buying a house; she was creating a new story for her family, one that would echo through generations.

Her children would grow up seeing homeownership as normal. They would understand building equity, making empowered financial decisions, and creating wealth through real estate not as foreign concepts but as natural parts of life. The mental block that had kept her family renting for generations had been shattered, replaced with a template of possibility.

Later that evening, Robin sent another message: "My mom cried when she saw the house. She said she never thought this would be possible for anyone in our family. But now my nieces are asking me to teach them about saving for their own homes someday. Can you believe it? It's really happening—we're changing the whole story."

That's the power of legacy work. One person's transformation becomes a beacon of possibility for an entire family system. Robin's journey from reluctant renter to proud homeowner wasn't just a personal victory; it was a revolution in her family's relationship with money and possibility, a new chapter in their generational story.

Her home is a testament to what's possible when we dare to write new money stories. But the real legacy isn't in the bricks and mortar; it's in the shift in consciousness that will ripple through her family for generations to come.

Sustaining Your Impact

Creating lasting change requires more than initial momentum. It demands sustained commitment and resilience in the face of challenges. As you continue your journey of financial transformation and legacy building, you'll encounter various forms of resistance, both internal and external. Family members might question your new approaches to money, old patterns may attempt to reassert themselves, and doubts could surface about the impact of your efforts. Understanding that these challenges are natural parts of the transformation process will help you navigate them more easily and wisely.

Handling resistance becomes an art form in itself. When others push back against your financial evolution, it often reflects their money wounds and fears rather than any shortcomings in your approach. Learning to hold space for their reactions while maintaining boundaries strengthens your resolve and impact. Rather than defending or justifying your choices, simply continue embodying your truth with compassion. Your consistent example speaks more powerfully than any argument could.

Navigating growth requires a delicate balance between pushing forward and allowing natural evolution. Some days, you'll feel strong momentum in your legacy work; other days may bring questions or uncertainty. This ebb and flow is not only normal but essential for sustainable transformation. Just as a tree needs growth spurts and consolidation periods to develop strong roots, your legacy work benefits from active expansion and quiet integration phases.

Building resilience becomes crucial for long-term impact. This means developing practices that sustain your energy and commitment, even when results aren't immediately visible. Regular reflection on the positive changes you've already created, celebrating small wins, and connecting with others on similar journeys can provide the emotional fuel needed for continued growth. Remember that your legacy work is a marathon, not a sprint—pace yourself accordingly.

Celebrating progress plays a vital role in sustaining momentum. Take time to acknowledge how far you've come, not just how far you have to go. Notice the subtle shifts in how your children talk about money, the growing financial confidence in your friends, or the ripples of change in your community. These observations aren't about ego. They're about recognizing the real impact of your transformation and drawing inspiration for continued growth.

Final Chapter Close

You've come so far in this journey—from understanding your money story to claiming your worth, from finding your voice to taking empowered action, from creating a vision to living integrated wealth. Yet perhaps the most beautiful part of this transformation is that it doesn't end with you. Every conscious choice you make, every boundary you honor, every example you set ripples outward in ways you may never fully see.

Your financial transformation has become a beacon of possibility for others. When you choose confidence over fear in money matters, you demonstrate what's possible. When you align your financial choices with your values, you show others they can do the same. When you speak openly about money with wisdom and compassion, you help heal generations of silence and shame around wealth.

This journey has equipped you with more than financial skills and knowledge; it's awakened a deeper understanding of your power to create positive change. You've discovered that true wealth isn't just about numbers in an account; it's about the richness of impact you make through conscious choices and aligned actions. Your money healing has become a gift that keeps giving, touching lives in seen and unseen ways.

As you continue forward, remember that your legacy isn't something waiting to happen in some distant future. It's being created every moment through your choices and actions. Each time you honor your worth, speak your truth about money or make an empowered financial decision, you're writing a new chapter not just in your own story but in the larger story of possibility you're creating for others.

The question now isn't "What's possible for me?" but "What's possible *through* me?" Your transformation has opened doors for your growth and the evolution of collective wealth consciousness. You've become a bridge between old patterns and new possibilities, between inherited limitations and emerging opportunities.

Remember that this ending is really a beginning. The principles and practices you've embraced become more powerful as you continue to embody them. Your impact grows stronger as you maintain your commitment to conscious wealth creation. The legacy you're building gains momentum with each aligned choice you make.

What legacy are you ready to live? The answer to this question will continue to evolve as you do. Trust that each step you take in alignment with your values and vision creates ripples of positive change. Your journey of financial transformation has become a light that illuminates new possibilities not just for you but for all whose lives you touch.

The future of wealth consciousness is shaped by people like you who dare to transform their relationship with money and share their journey with others. As you move forward, know that your financial healing and growth serve a purpose far greater than personal gain—they contribute to the healing and empowerment of the collective.

Step boldly into this ongoing journey of impact and transformation. Your legacy is alive in every conscious choice you make. The possibilities you're creating extend far beyond what you can see. Trust in the power of your example, the wisdom of your journey, and the ripples of transformation you're creating through your lived legacy.

KEY TAKEAWAYS:
- Legacy is lived forward, not just left behind
- Your transformation impacts generations
- Daily choices create lasting impact
- Teaching happens through example

Your Money Confidence Code: A Personal Wealth Identity Statement

By now, you realize that your financial success is not just about numbers—it's about the beliefs, behaviors, and commitments you choose to live by. Your Money Confidence Code is a personal declaration that aligns your mindset with your financial goals. Instead of allowing old money patterns to define you, you will write your own code—one that supports the wealth and confidence you deserve.

Step 1: Identify Your Core Money Values

Choose three words that best describe how you want to feel about money:

- Abundant
- Confident
- Strategic
- Secure
- Aligned
- Empowered
- Free
- In Control
- Expansive
- Grounded

Example: *"I want to feel confident, free, and aligned with my money."*

Step 2: Define Your Money Commitments

Complete the following sentences based on how you want to show up financially:

- I choose to believe that money is *(Example: "A tool for freedom, not a source of stress.")*

- I commit to *(Example: "Making financial decisions from a place of confidence, not fear.")*

- I release *(Example: "The belief that I have to work harder to be worthy of wealth.")*

- I am open to *(Example: "Receiving and managing larger amounts of money with ease.")*

Step 3: Write Your Money Confidence Code

Now, put it all together. This is your personal Money Confidence Code—the beliefs and commitments you will live by.

Example: *"I am a confident, free, and aligned wealth-builder. Money is a tool for freedom, not a source of stress. I commit to making financial decisions from a place of confidence, not fear. I release the belief that I have to work harder to be worthy of wealth, and I am open to receiving and managing money with ease."*

This is your new financial identity. This is the code you will live by.

About the Author

Janeil Pierre is a transformational Financial Confidence Expert, creator of The Confidence Money Method™, and author of The Money Confidence Code.

With a unique blend of practical financial expertise and soul-level transformation, Janeil empowers high-achieving professionals and entrepreneurs to build wealth while honoring their worth. A retired United States Army Sergeant First Class, Janeil's approach bridges the gap between financial knowledge and confidence, guiding clients to align their money decisions with their deepest values and create lasting financial freedom.

Janeil's story is one of extraordinary resilience and transformation. From living hand to mouth in her twenties to discovering financial literacy during her military journey, she rose to financial freedom and success while serving in the Army. However, her path wasn't without hardship. A traumatic spine injury and brain injury forced her to retire early, leading to profound personal challenges. Through her determination to heal mentally, physically, and emotionally, Janeil emerged stronger, using her experiences to guide others through life's toughest financial and emotional hurdles.

Today, as a Neuro-Transformational Life Coach, Speaker, and Financial Coach, Janeil combines her expertise in financial systems with her understanding of mindset and self-worth. Her signature programs, coaching, and speaking engagements have transformed thousands of lives by helping people break free from financial stress, rebuild their confidence, and step into their purpose, and her 2025 book debut will build on that impact. Janeil's work is a testament to her belief that no matter your past, you can create a fulfilling, abundant, and breathtakingly beautiful life.

Invitation to Work With Me

Ready to Take Your Money Confidence to the Next Level?

Congratulations! You've just completed *The Money Confidence Code*, and you're now equipped with the mindset shifts, tools, and strategies to transform your financial future. But if you're ready for personalized guidance, deep breakthroughs, and a step-by-step plan tailored to your unique goals, then private coaching may be the next best step for you.

Private Coaching with Janeil Pierre

This is an exclusive opportunity to work one-on-one with Janeil Pierre, the creator of **The Confident Money Method**™, and get direct, personalized support to:

- Identify and eliminate the hidden money blocks holding you back.
- Build a sustainable wealth strategy that aligns with your lifestyle.
- Make confident, empowered financial decisions without stress.
- Step fully into your financial power and create lasting abundance.

Who This Is For:

- High-achieving professionals and entrepreneurs who are ready to break free from financial stress.
- Those who earn a decent income but want to master it and confidently grow their wealth.

- Anyone committed to transforming their financial habits, beliefs, and systems once and for all.

How to Apply:

Private coaching spots are limited; this opportunity is available only by application. If you're serious about taking control of your financial future and working directly with Janeil, apply today to determine if this program is the right fit for you.

Apply now at: bit.ly/applythroughmcc or scan the QR code below.

Your financial transformation starts here. Let's make it happen together.

Acknowledgements

I want to acknowledge a few people without whom this book would not be possible.

First and foremost, to my mother, thank you. You ensured my home, meals, and laundry were taken care of while I spent endless hours pounding away at my keyboard over the past five years. From my Army transition to completing my Master's degree to launching my business and now this book—you've been my rock.

Ma, I know I get lost in my work, and it may not always seem like I appreciate you. But please know: nothing you do for me goes unnoticed or unappreciated. Thank you for standing by me on this rollercoaster called entrepreneurship.

Thank you to my coaches, Lisa Nichols, Jack Canfield, Sean Smith, and Zakiya Gradney. I don't think I have the right words to fully express the impact you've had on my life and career. Your guidance, belief in me, and willingness to pour into my purpose have changed me forever.

To my financial coach, Dr. Franchelle Ceasar, words can't fully express how much your grace, insight, and belief in me shifted my life and my business. Thank you for holding space for me and supporting this book from concept to reality. You are truly one of the best humans on this planet.

To my accountability partners and peer coaches, Dr. Francine Wingster, Rhona Bennett, Jenn Bertrand, Gentry Bohm, Hanna Essenburg, Candice Rawls, and the entire crew—thank you for picking me up when I was down, holding me when I couldn't hold myself, and encouraging me when I wanted to give up. Your presence has been a critical part of my healing journey.

To my besties and soul sisters, Morgan, Wendy, Suzie, Rhonda, Nicola, Allyson, Naomi, and Nargiz—thank you for loving me through every high and every breakdown. I know I can be...me, AKA a lot sometimes. But you all love me anyway. We truly have the kind of friendship people dream of.

To Dr. Denise Nicholson and the Bold Publishing Team—thank you. You lifted so much off my plate and ensured this book found its way into readers' hands. I couldn't have done this without you.

And finally, to everyone who pre-ordered this book the moment I announced it: You brought tears to my eyes. You didn't know what the pages held, but you believed in the message and me. That kind of support is beyond anything I could ever express.

From the depths of my heart—thank you, thank you, thank you.